REVEALING RESILIENT LEADERSHIP

PRAISE FOR DR. CYNTHIA CLAUSON

Revealing Resilient Leadership is the perfect roadmap for school leaders looking to transform and build capacity for meaningful change in their schools and districts. Throughout, Dr. Clauson shares powerful concepts and personal insights into those key elements needed to build strong, sustainable, and resilient schools. A great resource and guidebook for school leaders, their teams, and staff!

— RICH MCBRIDE, ED.D

So much of what Cynthia writes about resonates for me as an educator – a former classroom teacher and administrator. How she speaks about collaboration and communication is critical to how I think about leadership. Our experiences living abroad and working in different cultural communities with different cultural contexts have been invaluable in helping us develop lenses to do work here in the United States, particularly with marginalized and minoritized students. This book is a must-read for education leaders.

— ERIN JONES, AUTHOR OF *BRIDGES TO HEAL US*

A noted problem in education is underscoring an intentional approach to embrace school improvement processes that lever long-term sustainability. *Revealing Resilient Leadership* attacks this by unpacking complex concepts in an approachable manner for leaders to apply immediately. Dr. Clauson's framework unwraps various leadership themes and improvement mechanisms that will lead to organizational and team coherence in an accelerated context. Presenting a model for leaders to be resilient and strategic with their tactics to promote meaningful transformation, this book is a much-needed text in the AC-Stage of Education for leaders of learning organizations to ensure we reach the vision of success for all.

— MICHAEL CONNER, ED.D. FOUNDER & CEO AGILE EVOLUTIONARY GROUP, CORP.

Revealing Resilient Leadership

Empowering Leaders to Transform Schools for Long-Term Success

Foreword By Ted Howard

DR. CYNTHIA CLAUSON, PH.D.

Khrusos Books

Spokane, WA, USA

Published 2023 by Khrusos Books.

Paperback ISBN: 979-8-9888849-0-3

E-Book ISBN: 979-8-9888849-1-0

DISCLAIMER

Editing: Andrae Smith, Jr.

Cover Design: Emily's World of Design

To my daughter, Kate Clauson, who is my greatest teacher. You taught me and your teachers that everyone needs individualized education to unveil their greatness.

CONTENTS

FOREWORD
BY TED HOWARD

"Leadership is about making others better as a result of your presence and making sure that impact lasts in your absence."

— SHERYL SANDBERG

In education, we are constantly faced with new demands and evolving circumstances. The pressure to adapt and innovate has never been greater as the disruptive impact of the COVID-19 pandemic has forced schools to respond to a myriad of concurrent challenges. From integrating remote learning and overcoming learning loss to identifying and reducing inequities within the system, schools and educators nationwide have been stretched to their limits. Coupled with mounting teacher workloads and mental health concerns, a renewed emphasis on standardized testing and technology integration further test the education landscape.

My career in education has spanned over twenty-five years, during which I've taken on various roles, from an instructional assistant and home school coordinator to a teacher, head teacher, high school assistant principal, principal, and president of the Principal Association for Seattle Public Schools (SPS). Born and raised in Seattle, I come from a long line of educators, and my dedication to the students and families of the Seattle Public School District has led me to return home as the Assistant Superintendent of Strategy and Climate for SPS.

As I observe the landscape today, we know more about education than at any other time in history. Yet even so, these barriers can feel insurmountable, leaving educators and administrators feeling overwhelmed and sometimes discouraged. We must have skilled leaders who can help us uncover our strengths and weaknesses that will allow us to have the courage to grow to become a leader who will impact the world that changes daily. We need leaders who can bring back strength, resilience, and hope to the education sector.

For this reason, I am honored to present this book by Dr. Cynthia Clauson. Cynthia is a leader who has walked alongside me, helping me discover latent talents and build self-confidence. When I saw myself as a product of an education system that took and didn't develop, she held the mirror to show me I am so much more. Her guiding hand is both gentle and firm (a steel hand in a velvet glove), recognizing where she may need to intervene but never missing an opportunity to push you in the direction you know you need to go.

As an educator, Cynthia's journey began on a small farm in Spokane, where she fearlessly tested the limits of life. Among the first limits she challenged was her physical strength, determined to match the boys in their pursuits despite being a girl. Running and jumping on skis right alongside them, she not only kept up but learned to surpass many of them, fostering a deep sense of confidence that blossomed into unyielding resilience. She was honing her skill at a very young age, asking why and how as she tried to understand the world. She would ask many questions about what she would see, how things were, and why people would make the decisions they had made. Her mom and dad were a tremendous impact, and the first filter for Cynthia to understand the world was not fair and that there are many twists in life's journey.

These twists helped Cynthia discover her talent in leadership. This has enabled her to become a servant leader. A servant leader sees others and their many talents, reflecting the beauty of a pearl and the journey it takes to become polished. Her deep faith has allowed her to walk this path seeing the gifts people have. This is not always easy to see because we usually want something. Cynthia's talent is that she is never seeking something; she is trying to help others see the unique talents they have hidden from themselves and others because the world has taken the shine away from their pearl.

She discusses in her book that when you are committed to your purpose, when you have applied yourself and begun demonstrating your readiness to reach for higher levels in your journey, a mentor will "tap" you. This tapping may come as a call to be taken under their wing, but I have found it does not stop there. Mentors like Cynthia keep tapping you to remind you of your skills, to push you forward, to say you've been ready, to push yourself... all because they see in you what you may not see yourself. They see in you the leader waiting to be revealed.

Revealing Resilient Leadership is a book about school improvement, and it highlights the importance of the right leadership needed to develop schools for greater and greater gains. It will guide you as you strive to transform yourself to lead with a servant's heart. Through your service, you will transform others.

When you read this book, you will discover the various skills you always had but had buried deep inside because of your past. As you develop skills, you will become resilient, build your voice, learn to shine brightly, and discover you were always a pearl reflecting the light of others.

Finally, through the pages of this book, you will discover that we are all in continuous improvement throughout our lives. You will learn to see all students and adults as they were meant to be seen—all perfect in our own right. We take time from our day-to-day journey to see the world and understand that we are only here briefly and must enjoy every moment.

I wholeheartedly endorse this book to all educators, administrators, and anyone passionate about driving positive change in the world of education. Cynthia's approach to leadership and school improvement will leave an indelible mark on your practice. As the caterpillar becomes the butterfly, this book will serve as your chrysalis as you become the leader who takes flight. You will be amazed at how you become resilient.

—Ted Howard, *Chief Accountability Officer for Seattle Public Schools*

PREFACE

I woke up to someone pounding on my door. It must have been around two or three o'clock in the morning because that was one of the times the Muslim citizens of Bahrain would get up to go pray at the mosque. So it wouldn't have been unusual to hear movement outside in the halls of the apartment building. This was different.

As I lay in bed, not fully awake, this noise felt loud and aggressive. Somebody wanted inside. But who? What could this be? One of my colleagues at the school where I worked would have called and told me if there was something I needed to know. As my mind became less hazy, I started praying that God would wrap himself around me like a white light. This was something I prayed frequently for safety. I can't say exactly how long the pounding went on for, but I remember falling asleep again and waking the next morning thinking, "Sheesh... what a bizarre dream."

It was April 2015, so the weather in Bahrain was hot. My staff and I had planned a pearl dive since we were on our day off, and we were all looking forward to being out on the boat. When I tried to leave my apartment to meet them, the door wouldn't open. The handle just turned around in a circle, completely broken. That's when I realized what I heard the previous night was not a dream. Someone *had* tried to get in, and I had been saved from them.

When the lady who had come to pick me up arrived, it became clear how severe the damage was. "What's happened here?" she said from outside the door.

"I can't get out," I said, "Can you go downstairs and ask them to get me out of here?"

The front desk clerk came up with who I assume was the locksmith. They got the door open quickly. We found it had broken into the deadbolt in the main frame instead of breaking open, and the front side of the door was smashed and bent all around the handle. Strangely the clerk and locksmith didn't seem at all surprised. All I could think was, "This really happened. It wasn't a dream..."

I guess I should tell you why I was in Bahrain in the first place.

From 2010 to 2013, I was going back and forth from Seattle to DC working on this important legal project I thought high school kids needed to prevent themselves from becoming homeless and jobless and from having trouble with the law—which was often the result of profiling. I was helping sell little books by an attorney named Amanda Dubois, whom I'd met while sitting on the Board for the Hope Foundation, founded by former Seattle Seahawk Mack Strong and his wife, Zoe Higheagle Strong. In the process, I met many wonderful people over three years in Alexandria, Virginia, and Washington, DC, and worked on amazing projects with fascinating people like Earth Wind and Fire Band as they supported Duke Ellington Performing Arts High School with our team of curriculum development leaders and grant writers, along with the producers who had introduced me to the Headmaster.

Eventually, I thought I would apply for a position in Mexico teaching fourth or fifth grade (because I wanted to learn Spanish), so I applied to the international schools program. The organizers said, "Oh no. We can't have you do that."

"Why?" I asked.

"Because you've been a US school administrator. We need you somewhere else." They then had me interview for a school in Al Wakra, Qatar, in the Middle East.

I didn't get that position, but some months later, the international school organizers called about an American International School opening in Doha, Qatar, that felt like a better fit (and it was right down the road from the first school).

Before I accepted, I spoke with my mom about it, and she said, "Oh, you have to go." I was shocked. She said, "Because you need to teach children to read in that part of the world in English. The mothers will learn to read in English and help us create world peace. They will teach their children how to protect each other and show respect for others because they don't want them to die."

I had never thought of it that way, but it felt right. When the offer came, I accepted. It was a good offer, too, for that kind of work, so I trusted it was the right decision. Just before I was meant to leave, my mother fell and broke her hip, and nine days later, she died. It was very hard for me because it was so sudden, and I wasn't sure that I should or even that I could go to the Middle East. Ultimately, I went knowing that I was doing what she really wanted me to do.

The Doha sheiks partnered me with George Dymond, an experienced administrator from the UN school in New York City, who was hired by Princeton and had been there a year already. He needed a leader who knew how to do the implementation of a school while he knew how to do all the work with the sheiks, who owned the school and oversaw its development and interests on behalf of the Emir of Qatar.

It was like an adventure but so, so meaningful, and I was so comfortable everywhere. I was surprised that I could be so comfortable in such a conservative Islamic culture, but I was. We were actually working with members of the Emir's family, and I met wonderful and talented people. One of my Al Muftah colleagues was an amazing principal who had developed British systems and was born in Ceylon. She was originally African, raised in Great Britain, and came from an impressive lineage of people who had started schools. And her school was right across the street from the original one I interviewed for.

Unfortunately, I injured my ankle not long after arriving. I did my best to keep functioning for as long as I could, but I had to return to the States for surgery. I never got to meet my teachers in their new setting because they were to arrive the day I flew home, and all I could think was, "Why, God?"

I had only been home about three months and was preparing for the surgery when I got a call from a woman in Bahrain. Her husband had been a support for superintendents and school leaders in the region for a long time, and my name had come up.

"You were recommended by the head of the Doha British schools, JC Chihuly," she said.

I told her about my leg, and all she said was to get it taken care of and then get out there. They needed me right away. I didn't get to stay in Doha, but it all seemed well-timed because I needed the surgery, and then I was needed elsewhere to continue the work I intended to do. So just eight weeks after my surgery, I flew to Bahrain.

It was a horrendous flight! I was wearing this huge, funny boot to protect my ankle and had to be pushed around in wheelchairs at the airport. I kept thinking, "Why am I doing this?" Of course, I knew why, but at the moment, it was so uncomfortable. Then I arrived in Bahrain.

The experience was so wildly like the Arabian Dream. It truly felt like royal treatment. They provided drivers and beautiful apartments with views of the Arabian Sea, just like in Doha, only there were people living there from all over the world. But my greatest joy was the simplicity and appreciation. I was grateful to be working there and to be received by them, and they were thankful that *I* was there—and the children truly loved going to school and having the opportunity to learn.

The staff that had been hired was so diverse! We had Americans, Brits, Canadians, South Africans, Bahrainis, Syrians, and some Nigerians, and I fell in love with working with them. I could not get rid of that feeling of immense contentment and joy every minute of the day from when I got up in the morning.

The people that interviewed me were all highly experienced in international school leadership and successful, and some were doctors—*women* with doctorates—and treated me with such regard, which was a very different attitude than I had experienced most recently in the US. The woman who had called me and asked me to come was nearly seventy years old and so vibrant, like she was just fifty. Everyone I worked with was like that; you wouldn't have known their ages. I thought, "Wow! How come we can't be like this more back home?"

The truth is these were people on a mission who shared one purpose and focused on not leading, helping, or overseeing but walking alongside the community. The goal was to work together, using everyone's unique expertise to bring out the community's talents, leadership, and gifts so that they could continue to lead their own school when we were gone. So we just did what we could do and shared with them what we knew how to do in the US. It created a synergy that I had never seen and results for which the school owners were so appreciative.

Dr. Mohammed and Mrs. K., who had founded and developed the school, were bringing education to the "middle-class professionals children" in the community. The Prince of Bahrain recognized them with an acknowledgment of their success. The school was also integrated, boys and girls, which was a particularly important part of my mission and similar to our goal at my first international school. They had a vision for what they wanted it to

be. They knew the values that were important to their stakeholders. You can imagine that not everyone agreed with this new
model of schooling, especially with non-Muslim foreigners part-
nering in it.

I had been treated so well by almost everyone and gotten so
comfortable that I never really thought of myself as stirring up
trouble, let alone being in danger. Until one night, I woke to a
pounding at my door... Someone tried to get into my apartment
that night. To this day, it's not clear who or why. All I could do
was try to keep to the mission and keep my head down. This event
was the trigger that eventually became a seed for this book.

My time in the Middle East taught me many things. First, it
showed me the importance of faith. This book is not about my
religion, but I want to note that my faith played a huge role in my
willingness to take on certain jobs, take risks and say, "OK." My
work there was some of the most fulfilling for more reasons than I
have space to list. It takes a lot of courage to take some assignments. Sometimes, in leadership, you know that if you take
certain roles, you will be stretched. You must find a way to see the
stretching as meaningful for those you will lead and support.

It also affirmed the importance of resilience when things
become challenging—and they *do* become challenging. Resilience
is a central theme of this book, and it's something I believe
everyone has to find for and within themselves. I was chosen
because I was qualified to handle unique and sometimes unpre-
dictable circumstances and stay cool under this pressure, a charac-
teristic of resilient leaders. As you progress through these pages,
you'll see again and again how this idea of resilience appears in
your work. The British adage comes to mind that we often say to
each other, "Keep calm and carry on."

Another important lesson I learned was what it means to be a
leader behind the curtains. In leadership, you want to know how

to be effective without needing to be front-and-center. At my evaluation, Mrs. K. made a point to tell me she and her husband recognized the work I had been doing and that they knew I was behind many of the successes, even though I had a talent for keeping my head down. This confirmed that leaders are not leaders because they have the title or the credit but because of their ability to walk alongside others to bring about their leadership skills and encourage ownership over their piece of the results.

This leads me to the most important takeaway I got from my time abroad: collaborative action is at the core of the most successful leadership and systems improvement models. I'll explain what collaborative action means later in the book, but the way we worked in Bahrain was one form. There was clear data to work from, the priorities were decided on by the stakeholders, and my staff and I were chosen for our specific skill sets and ability to lead different parts of the process. Everyone had skin in the game and felt like they were part of something bigger. When this happens, engagement goes up, and so do results. If it could work in this international school in a different culture, it could certainly work in the United States.

If nothing else, the night I woke to my door being kicked in brought me a lot of clarity. My physical safety may have been in real danger. But in another way, it was a night when I woke up to what I was really living for, and I was reminded of the need to follow my calling of service. That is why I am writing this book now, to continue being of service in helping address some opportunities here on our shores, in our districts. There are economic disparities, accessibility disparities, literacy, and opportunity disparities because many school districts are not pushing the boundaries of what they can do, and it is the children who suffer. Their parents bring them to us like treasure, precious pearls, and we must take care of them. Unfortunately, some places are slow to adapt to modern needs, and children are slipping through the cracks.

I've written this book because I believe in schools where students don't slip, where there are interventions and measures against it, where all members of a professional learning community (PLC) can work toward that common goal. This type of vision takes change agents capable of initiating direction and seeing it through, and that's what I hope to equip readers of this book to do. This story is for the future of our children and our educators to build a better tomorrow for all of us.

1

INTRODUCTION

"The journey of a thousand miles begins with one step."

— LAO TZU

This book had taken many shapes before landing on what it is now. Initially, I thought it would be titled, *A Woman Revealed* and focus on revealing the challenges faced by women and minoritized leaders. The idea was that by "uncovering" myself, I could show future leaders how to be just a little more resilient. The problem with that was that this book was supposed to also be a guide to leadership for school improvement, and it would need more focus to be of much use.

During the process, it became about school improvement strategy, building on the work of Charles Salina, Suzann Girtz, and Joanie Eppinga—and in a way, it still is. In 2016, Salina, Girtz, and Eppinga published their first book, *Powerless to Powerful: Leadership for School Change* (2016), detailing their school improvement model of the same name (P2P for short). They provided a "new way of thinking and leading," as it was put in the book's Introduction, centered around high expectations, community, and trust. It is a collaborative model that I've come to know well through testing and implementation at multiple sites. Much of what I have to share is related to this, as you'll see in the book.

However, that was not enough.

Ultimately, what I wanted to contribute was neither the elements of leadership nor school improvement strategy, but a path to both—a leadership framework with a focus on improving achievement in schools. Grounded in collaborative action research models and drawing from my experience, what I offer is centered on the characteristics and tools necessary to be the leader that can drive change from within. This is where resilience comes in.

When we say a word often enough, we take for granted that we know what it means. We take "resilient" to mean sturdy or strong when, in reality, it means enduring or lasting. There is implied friction or tension within the word itself. A resilient leader can endure and press forward toward results, even against opposition. Sometimes the opposition is circumstantial, like not having the funding or necessary school supplies. Other times, it's personal, like team members and stakeholders not aligning with the vision. To be an effective change leader, you must be able to stand in those waters without getting swept up and keep moving forward, sometimes against the tide.

So, in this book, I provide three things that I believe you will need to become the leader who endures: stories, mindsets, and tools. Each chapter includes a story or example from my career so you can see the concepts in action, and I present the most vital lessons and mindsets that impact the outcomes. Last, I break down a distinct element of the collaborative action model as it was employed so that you can take it and implement it in your work.

Here is your first tool. To help you better understand the

meaning of resilience in the pages to come, I want you to consider the following graphic and hold it in your mind as you read:

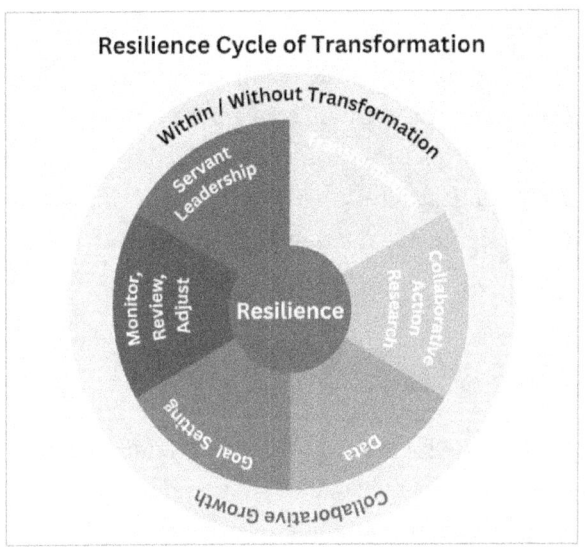

(Figure 1: Resilience Cycle of Transformation)

Coming into this book, you may envision achieving transformation as a logical result. However, I invite you to view transformation through a new lens: it is not merely an endpoint but a continuous process. Throughout our discussion of the continuous improvement framework, you will come to understand that growth is an iterative, cumulative, and shared journey guided by the right leadership. This journey relies on key components like data, collaborative action research, and monitoring systems to measure progress, all of which require a leader who fosters shared leadership.

While this is not itself a novel concept, I want to emphasize the importance of resilience in this process. In order to transform your learning organization, you must reflect the light of others within your team. This means embracing a collaborative role within the circle rather than being at the center. It means holding the vision and working diligently to eliminate barriers until everyone else is on board. It means cultivating resilience to stay steadfast in your pursuit of a higher purpose.

The beauty of transformation lies in the reciprocal nature of its impact. As you transform your team, they transform you. This is the essence of within/without transformation—a shared growth process that nurtures more leaders within the system, creating a more stable organization. When the time comes for you to move to your next assignment, there will be no fear that the system will crumble, as it, too, will have developed resilience.

WHO IS THIS BOOK FOR?

I've written this book primarily for school administrators who are struggling to close achievement gaps and create environments where all students can flourish. However, as you'll come to know, the frameworks presented here can work at any level and across industries. Whether you're a principal, a district superintendent, or a leader in another type of organization, your goal will be to create or maintain a system designed for continual improvement based on triangulated and viable quantitative and qualitative data, and that is what I'm presenting here in this book.

This book also aims to aid new-to-role and training administrators in developing the skills to continue up the ladder. As a woman leader who's worked seamlessly in diverse communities, I know firsthand what challenges women and marginalized people face. I believe this also gives me a little perspective on the importance of representation. More children and families need representation in these challenging times, strong female role models and models of their own cultures to address the need to stay the course.

WHY IS NOW THE TIME FOR THIS BOOK?

Our American society has increasingly pointed the way through the issues with schools and family needs during the pandemic and the issues around immigration and citizenship. There has been an increasing focus on schools needing to be a haven amid the crisis and grappling with maintaining the role of productive places for families and their children.

School staff need a guide and leader who is alongside them more than in front of them. The community needs the schools to keep the role of a safe and supportive place for their families and children while increasing the opportunities for youth to become productive citizens in our society. This guide is born out of a career that has required resilience in the face of barriers; resourcefulness amid tight and turbulent times; and respect across diverse cultures, communities, and continents. I believe it is an important focus for leaders today to know they can go down in the fire and rise again from the ashes to keep serving children and society through school leadership roles.

I've had a truly rich and diverse experience throughout my career, filled with diverse people and many kinds of positions. They've given me countless opportunities to grow and learn, and I'm writing this book because I truly believe there were some nuggets of gold that could help other people looking to walk a similar path as mine—like the first article that I wrote with my colleague Melodee Loshbaugh called "Turning Straw Into Gold" (1988).

My experience might help others find the same joy that I found amid difficult times and to remain resilient when things were challenging. My words may provide them with guides and pieces of truth that resonate with them so well that they take their next steps forward in their decision-making. They may continue to help other people and respond to the needs in our society that are across diversity. Maybe I would help build a bridge across the divides of the differences of people and help developing leaders ponder other ways of doing things than the ones that automatically come to our mind and discern that there are options. And the option is to jump in with both feet knowing you will eventually rise to the top.

WHAT SHOULD YOU EXPECT?

This book is divided into eleven chapters, each exploring another aspect of resilient leadership and the school improvement model. Here is a preview of the principles we'll be discussing:

In Chapter 2, you will explore servant leadership, a philosophy that prioritizes serving others over personal gain or organizational success. By understanding the principles of servant leadership, you can apply them in your educational setting to create an environment for growth and development, foster collaboration, and have a positive impact on others.

Chapter 3 delves into transformational leadership, which goes beyond servant leadership by developing future leaders and fostering a culture of shared leadership. You will learn about the characteristics and practices of transformational leaders and how you can inspire others, create a shared vision, and drive innovation and growth in your educational organization.

Continuing in Chapter 4, you will come to know the continuous improvement cycle, an ongoing process that enables progress in your educational setting. By understanding the components of the cycle, you will be equipped to monitor progress, address challenges, and foster a culture of resilience and shared ownership, all for the benefit of student learning.

Chapter 5 introduces the concept of creative tension as a dynamic force that drives innovation. You will learn how to bridge the gap between your PLC's current reality and desired outcomes by harnessing the power of creative tension.

In Chapter 6, the focus shifts to emphasizing the importance of intentional and targeted strategies. This chapter provides practical guidance on implementing laser-focus strategies, collaborating effectively, and monitoring progress to meet the unique needs of your students.

Chapter 7 explores the significance of partnerships in education and embracing cultural diversity. Collaborating with various stakeholders, such as schools, educators, students, families, community organizations, and businesses, is vital for creating inclusive and supportive learning environments. This chapter highlights the importance of establishing successful partnerships and embracing cultural diversity to enhance the educational experience and create a positive impact on individuals and communities.

Chapter 8 and Chapter 9 highlight the fundamental aspects of effective collaboration in education: community voice and group goal-setting. Embracing community voice and collaboratively defining shared objectives ensure that your collaborative endeavors align with the needs and aspirations of your educational community.

In Chapter 10, you will explore the role of mentoring. This chapter provides insights into the value of mentorship in your development and your role as a mentor, fostering a culture of growth and development within your educational organization.

Finally, Chapter 11 discusses how effective leaders hand off leadership to the next leader. You will understand what it means to be a resilient leader and build resilience into your organization.

RESILIENCE INSIGHTS

- Resilience is at the center of this transformation process. If you think of this cycle like a bicycle wheel, then transformation and collaborative growth are like the rim, the other six components are the spokes, and resilience is the hub where they all connect. Together, they create the stability that allows the wheel to keep turning.

2

WHY THE "SERVANT" LEADER?

"Servant-leadership is a leadership philosophy in which the goal of the leader is to serve. This is different from traditional leadership, where the leader's main goal is the thriving of their organization or company. A servant-leader shares power, puts the needs of the employees first and helps people develop and perform as highly as possible. Instead of the people existing to serve the leader, the leader exists to serve the people."

— SEN SENDJAYA & JAMES C. SARROS

There has never been a more critical time for strong leadership to arise in education. The impact of the COVID-19 pandemic on schools and student achievement has been drastic, and though administrators and educators worked hard to rebound and secure a tourniquet above the proverbial wound, the extreme conditions exposed and exacerbated many existing issues in the school systems. On the brighter side, it also revealed the important role school districts have in holding together and uplifting their communities. Looking ahead, we're obligated not only to find equilibrium or a return to "normal."

As stewards of the community, it is on us to address the issues and help every student thrive—even beyond the recent health crisis. Because the idea of leaders as servants is so important to how we will approach continual improvement in this book, it felt appropriate to begin by clarifying how a servant leader appears and why the qualities they embody are so invaluable.

ORIGINS OF THE SERVANT LEADER

"Servant leadership is a philosophy and set of practices that enriches the lives of individuals, builds better organizations and ultimately creates a more just and caring world."

—Robert K. GreenLeaf (1977)

Robert Greenleaf's definition of servant leadership and the key characteristics of this type of leader are highly effective when coupled with total quality management (TQM) and continuous improvement cycles because the directive is to support human growth and potential of the staff and the students. According to Greenleaf's essentials of servant leadership, being a leader is about helping people develop and grow so they can contribute to the overall growth of the organization. Through their high performance and increased ownership of the results, they function as leaders as well. More importantly, Greenleaf asserts, "a servant can only be a leader as long as the person remains a servant" (1977). By the very nature of serving and invoking the purpose of service, the leader can create transformational leadership and ethical decision-making practices across the organization, and through others' participation, this will develop those who are serving as servant leaders.

For Greenleaf, the idea of a leader as a servant emerged after reading *Journey to the East*, by Herman Hesse. In this story, the central figure, a man named Leo, accompanies a party on a journey. Leo is a servant who does their menial chores but who also sustains them with his spirit and his song. All goes well on the journey while Leo is with them as their servant. When he disappears, the group falls into disarray, and the journey is abandoned. They realize they cannot make it without him.

After some years of wandering, the chief leader of the party discovers Leo has been taken into the order that has sponsored the journey. In this place, he learns that Leo, whom he first knew as a servant, was, in fact, the leader of the order. Leo becomes a guiding spirit, a great and noble leader. He serves as a leader, inspiring people all over the world to enter the process of personal transformation. Through the listening and learning process, they become transformational leaders as well.

Out of this enlightened perspective, Greenleaf developed the conceptual framework of servant leadership, also known as transformational leadership. (There is a minor distinction between the two, which I will elaborate in the next chapter.) The servant leadership theory is based on ten characteristics listed in his book, *Servant Leadership: A Journey into the Nature of Legitimate Power and Greatness* (1977). They are:

- Listening
- Empathy
- Healing
- Awareness
- Persuasion
- Conceptualization
- Foresight
- Stewardship
- Commitment to the growth of people
- Building community

These are not simply traits possessed by the leader. They're a spiritual, ethical, and moral approach intended to treat personality variables optimistically, suggesting that each trait, when developed, will determine the effects of leadership. Greenleaf based his theory on these personality traits and developed the foundation of an ethical perspective on leadership that identifies key moral behaviors that leaders must continuously show to make progress.

The best testament of Greenleaf's ethical foundation is when the ends for action are developed and embedded as common language and traits in the organization, viewable in its members while they are involved in daily activities like decision-making, monitoring results, and planning for future goals. It is important to note that Servant leadership presupposes that collaborative engagement is a precursor to increased results and the desire to take part in the team and work toward shared outcomes.

As a leader in more than one instance, I have found that I must first seek to understand those I serve or lead (Stephen Covey, 2016). This translates to being the lead listener and learner. I have learned that leading with transparency and inclusive practice increases the likelihood, mutual understanding, and trust between those who are led and makes the difference between the number of those who choose to take part and those who choose not to participate. Now, it is my intention that by sharing the stories and steps of continuous improvement through this lens that you will reflect on Greenleaf's perspective while critically thinking to take action for organizational situations and problems.

"GOOD TROUBLE"

We look at the leaders that emulate these traits—those who are seeking to follow moral and ethical leadership of service with Greenleaf's lens—and be the mirrors we hold for each other as we walk alongside one another, develop, and transform. I have not only been fortunate to work with several leaders who have promoted this type of leadership and held the mirror for me to reflect on my leadership and refine my skills to be a servant leader. Most significantly, I have been trained by Dr. Shirley Holloway, who was not only instrumental to me in developing excellence in leadership. It was because of her leadership that she was recognized by the American Association of School Administrators (AASA) and in Alaska as Superintendent of the Year and could continue the excellence loop by developing greatness in diverse leaders throughout her career.

As the foundational premise, servant leaders all have a desire to attain the ten basic characteristics and strive to develop these traits in others. One of the most important traits of a servant leader who remains resilient through the waves of difficulties in leadership management is to persevere and stay the course in the face of adversity. The traits necessary to sustain in the same or similar profession are patience and courage. Not passive patience, but active patience. For me, a person who stands out with active patience and stick-to-itiveness is Congressman John Lewis.

John Lewis spoke often about being at the crucial life point on the Selma bridge and about having to be patient with the people. In his book, *Across That Bridge: A Vision for Change and the Future of America* (2017), he talks about forgiving in order to continue staying the course, even while he was despised and beaten to where most people would have walked or crawled away defeated. He carried on, patient and courageous in the face of that hatred, and became a phenomenal national leader in the US House of Representatives.

Lewis contributed as a servant and kept the dream alive, staying "in good trouble" while keeping the focus of an ethical servant connected to the aim of transforming society and the betterment of life for all those he served. All the while relying on his faith in a higher purpose and keeping his calling as a guiding compass for many followers. Most importantly, he was not passive. He exhibited a focus on the common good along with the development of community, stewardship, and foresight for community growth, and he maintained an active engagement to bring people to a sense of higher moral, ethical, economic, and spiritual good as they became leaders of the social justice movement.

Applying this approach to the teams I have led, the three most prominent characteristics I have taken from John Lewis's example are **ethical choices, patience,** and **courage.** They become most evident and necessary when what you must do in service is right but not always popular. During moral dilemmas, I have found that foremost, a leader must do the right thing, which is to be ethical and model patience and courage in the face of adversity. And second, by exhibiting strength, staying the course when others fall away, makes a servant stand out and continue to collect followers of like minds, ripe for building transformational and collaborative communities.

The byproduct is the transformation of good stewards. Of course, when the leader stays the course to make things better for children and families it is worth staying patient with dissenting people and even standing alone in the fire. Like John Lewis, you must stay focused on doing what is right, honorable, and just in all circumstances. This may put you at risk, or require hard sacrifices at times. Lean into your faith and remain encouraged that you are doing the right thing for the right reasons.

If I had one reflection to impress upon you from my career, it would be to remember that it isn't enough to just serve what people want. You lead toward the highest principles of service, first, by making crooked paths straight and holding the candle to light the path behind and ahead. Second, you point in the right direction to bring people into the work so that together you make the paths straight for new followers, creating new leaders in the process. Some people will not agree or resist the arc you are creating. A servant leader must pick the best course of action and then stay calm and carry on in the face of adversity.

Some of the other leaders that come to mind as examples of this type of leader on a world stage are Gandhi, Mother Teresa, Dr. Martin Luther King Jr., and Nelson Mandela. As with John Lewis, these high-profile leaders knew their purpose, leading many years through suffering and criticism, steadfastly modeling their ideal of service to their people and a higher sense of justice. I have found personally in leading you cannot let that disruption or disagreement from those served dissuade you from your purpose. The dissenters cannot detract you from the common good. As for any servant leader, and it is just as true for me, you will always be just the shell or vessel in which the Spirit worked.

That is the humility of just knowing we are just human beings on this planet being worked through by a much greater spirit, representing the greater good. By working in this spirit or intention, many times, the results are greater than could be created by and for oneself. With this mindset, John Lewis did not personalize the adversity but used it to fuel his cause and fulfill his purpose. History will show he didn't have to stand out to be somebody important; rather, he became important by being patient, courageous, and not quitting.

BRIDGING THE DIVIDE

A servant leader stands apart from the spotlight of a central figure. Instead, they operate as a "leader behind the curtain," quietly guiding individuals. This leadership style can be challenging in the present because it emphasizes collaboration, and those being led may not always align with your direction. They may employ passive or aggressive resistance, tempting you to revert to a top-down approach. However, it's essential to recognize that a leader's strength lies in the collective power of their team. Success requires many hands and like-minded individuals working together. As the Algonquin Table of leadership illustrates, the focus cannot be on the leader alone. Rather, it involves empowering and instilling courage in the entire team, nurturing growth and shared influence.

Many times throughout my career, I have faced the delicate balance of representing the education environment, serving both the internal organizational team and the families and community at large. If there's one thing I've learned, it is that great success is always collaborative. Listening and communication have been key in recognizing the voices of internal and external stakeholders and finding common ground to improve and fulfill the destiny of the children we shared. Then a leader can help to build "bridges" as Erin Jones so clearly speaks of in *Bridges to Heal US* (2021).

What Robert Greenleaf shares about listening and compassion is like Erin's message of "building a bridge." We must bring disparate voices to the table and come to a common understanding of what is just and fair. If I may invoke a sense of urgency, it is necessary for the survival of humanity as we know it. We cannot spend our time splitting hairs and pointing fingers while doing what we have always done in the past to establish camps because there are huge issues that impact all of us. We can't win this battle alone: we must stand together.

Since I have spent my forty-two-year-long career analyzing and surveying the leadership in schools, I have wondered and marveled at the essential role of public schools. During the COVID-19 pandemic, the educators and education system carried families' meals and continued to serve their children's education while adapting and learning how to remotely serve. The essential role in the stability of our country was impressive! However, with time, other social challenges became apparent.

At the national level, we saw the infighting in response to a pandemic—people who refused to vaccinate against those who said we must vaccinate to protect all people; people who refused to be forced to wear a mask against those who believed wearing them was essential to protecting the common good. It was a conflict of personal liberty versus the common good, a perspective I never thought I would see exist. As a servant leader, it was my job to protect and model the protection of others. The choice to say it was not my responsibility to care for others was never in my mindset, never.

This divisiveness was nothing short of identity politics, reflecting the cultural challenge we faced in the US. During this time, we saw many types of leaders, but few on the national stage who consistently put the needs of their constituents over what was more appealing to their respective audiences. As I said, what is right is not always popular. A leader who is a good steward must be informed and act in the best interests of all parties. This was missing in the beginning of the pandemic. People need to be able to rely on the servant to look out for the best interests of everyone to feel safe and share their voice in the service of resolution for all. A servant leader invites continued conversation and manages emotion through compassion and listening. This builds trust, which is essential to ongoing collaborative action. (We'll talk about this more throughout the book.)

In the State of Washington, my observation is that our educators and administrators saw themselves as servants. Under all the different views, their purpose was to serve the community and the children and to be whatever that took. This meant relying on medical data and scientific guidance so that all protocols were evidence-based. This meant maintaining transparency through proactive communication. This meant relying on collaborative activity and distribution of resources, training, and personnel between districts so that students and families got what they needed to feel safe and weather the storm.

In the leaders I encountered, there was not an ego-based, self-focused response, not even after the crisis subsided, they went on as always serving the children and community, so no one got lost. I am proud to say that happened from community to community. It truly was "all hands on-deck," like during a world crisis such as wartimes. I was so proud of the State of Washington and its educators. Servant leadership, as exemplified through the pandemic, is about doing what is necessary and putting what is right and truly important (the well-being of others) before rank, title, pride, and politics.

The COVID-19 crisis set the scene as a good place to have a servant conversation as the characteristics of this type of leadership articulated by Robert Greenleaf were exhibited in this crisis and to weather the extended period of isolation. The leaders in each community, if they were doing a responsive job, exhibited listening, empathy, and the responsibility for healing the community. As a result, we continued to prepare the children and families for whatever was coming next. The lessons of communication, mobilization, and innovation created momentum for changes in the future delivery of education as we know it. So even though the process was tumultuous, and there were many divergent voices, we learned there can be something new and better, and we will survive along with possibly thriving. Out of this crisis, those servant leaders have become patient, courageous, and collaborative mentors to the community. They became resilient.

Altogether, I want to reaffirm that servant leadership is not about crisis-management but showing up ready to give of yourself. It recognizes that power and responsibility are intrinsically linked, and one cannot assume responsibility for others without knowing them, hearing them, and making space for them. It is about decentering yourself so that the community can rise. Through your example, you will not only guide your organization to empower leaders who can and will serve, you will identify your place in time. Over this book, I will share various concepts about leadership and resilience, and it is your imperative to ground them in the knowledge that leaders exist to serve the highest good of their communities.

RESILIENCE INSIGHTS

- Resilience is exemplified in the servant leader's ability to endure challenges and difficulties while putting the needs of others first. A resilient servant leader maintains their commitment to service even in the face of adversity, fostering an environment of growth and development.
- Resilient leaders stand their ground and stay committed to their principles, even when met with dissenting voices or resistance. This resilience empowers them to weather challenges while remaining steadfast in their ethical choices.
- Resilient servant leaders are skilled at building bridges between diverse perspectives and finding common ground. They navigate conflicts with resilience, fostering collaboration and unity. Their ability to persevere and lead through disagreements showcases their resilience in promoting the common good.

3
TRANSFORMATIONAL LEADERSHIP

"Leadership is communicating people's worth and potential so clearly that they come to see it themselves."

— STEPHEN R. COVEY

In the previous chapter, we unpacked the concept of servant leadership and its importance in the success of an organization. Servant leaders put the needs of the people they serve above their own egos and prioritize the success of the organization over their personal status or gain. This leadership style is characterized by collaboration and teamwork, where the leader acts as a facilitator for the collective success of the group.

However, as shown by the story of Leo, even the most effective servant leader may not be enough to create a lasting impact. When the leader is no longer present, the organization may struggle to function and maintain its success. This is where the concept of **transformational leadership** comes into play.

Transformational leadership goes beyond the principles of

servant leadership by not only putting the needs of the people first but also acknowledging the importance of developing future leaders. A transformational leader recognizes the need for growth and development within the organization and actively works to create a culture of leadership at all levels. By doing so, the leader serves the organization and empowers others to do the same.

This is essential to creating resilience within the organization and the direction it is trying to go. Transformational leaders, therefore, not only set a good pace for their teammates but act as mentors all along.

We're really talking about transforming the organization at a foundational level. Our focus is not on creating specific outcomes but on creating the infrastructure for setting appropriate priorities, analyzing data, and initiating a continuous improvement cycle. Transformational leaders accomplish this through what's called second-order change.

SECOND-ORDER CHANGE

When people think of leadership and organizational change, they usually envision what's called first-order change, where leaders make changes to processes, systems, or structures within an organization. What we're talking about with transformational leadership is really second-order change. This is a more profound level of transformation that involves a shift in an organization's values, beliefs, and culture, and it requires a leader who can inspire and empower their followers to embrace new ways of thinking and behaving.

To successfully lead second-order change, transformational leaders are not only transacting by asking someone to do something but also adept at guiding their people through personal and collective growth, helping them develop the skills and attitudes necessary to drive the change forward. How they act and create change and how they involve people in the change process collaboratively, respectfully, and inclusively is how second-order change works.

You can think of second-order change leader's thought process more like this: "I'm going to set the conditions for change. I will help support the discovery through awareness opportunities and analysis of various forms of data to explore what transpires in the organization, and collaboratively we will create the future and the changes we want to see." A leader encourages the transformation process by asking questions and posing scenarios. For example, a leader might say, "I would like to see the vision going in a broader direction. What do you think?" This style invites people to the table and is the essence of the transformational process.

Thomas Sergiovanni was one of the first researchers to really talk about transformational leadership compared to transactional leadership. He described second-order change and how within this process, leaders are no longer looking at just identifying a singular data point and saying, "We have changed by this data point, and that's what the results should be measured by" (1996). Instead, he outlines that a transformational leader looks at a full circle of continuous improvement (plan, act, do, revise). They oversee an iterative process based on assessment, action, review, and adjustment in which every team member takes ownership of some element of the project.

Moreover, leaders do not merely direct their team members in this process. Transformational leadership happens through mirroring. A Japanese practice known as Aikido is a good representation of this concept. Instead of being like two boxers facing and countering each other blow-for-blow, in Aikido, as one person moves, the other person moves with them. That's the mirror; as your team moves, you move with them. You don't come at them; this is transacting or transactional leadership. You want to move with each person so they work in harmony toward a shared desired outcome together.

Here's an example of how this might look. Let's say that you're a brand-new leader in an organization. All everyone knows is the process and the systems. What might be the first thing for you to consider if you want to be a transformational leader versus a transactional leader? Because you're running a change process, your goal is to find what needs transformation instead of preserving the status quo. The minute you start considering the processes and systems, along with the impact on the adult and student learners and input from all stakeholders, you're moving away from transacting and toward transforming.

The process begins with the questions. What is working? Where is the organization off track? Who is on the team, and what do they think the priorities are? Who's performing well in their role, and how can you help others perform at their best?

So, a transformational leader, in that circumstance, would get to know their team members. When you have people who are good in their departments, for instance, your first act should not be to move them away from that. You already know where they are doing well, and you want to keep them there. Get to know who the teachers are, what they are good at, their strengths, and where they need to grow at a grade level.

Schools can become places that create systems where they grow leaders and refine and encourage the talents of the people. Think of it like a department store. Let's say somebody's fantastic over in the technology department, somebody else is over here in toys, and someone else excels in clothing. It's much easier to align team members to their strengths. In a learning environment, this creates opportunities for the children to be exposed to adults with gifts that best match them.

As it pertains to continuous improvement, this extends beyond keeping literature masters in the English department. You may have an English teacher who specializes in teaching and testing for critical thinking and a math teacher who trained as a systems engineer. Your science department head may have a background in government contracting. When you are beginning new initiatives, knowing these strengths can help you align team members with work that best fits their ability to contribute to the larger mission.

POWERLESS TO POWERFUL

Hopefully, it is clear to you that transformational leadership is about empowerment. In transactional styles of leadership, everyone feels like their hands are tied, like direction is given to them often on top of and without regard to the barriers they already face. In this type of system, input from team members is deprioritized compared to tasks and goals set by incoming, often detached, leaders. The result is that team engagement drops because they have no ownership or sway over the decisions. When this happens, growth halts, and the organization loses momentum and resilience, becoming effectively powerless.

As a transformational leader, your goal is to shift your PLC from a state of powerlessness to empowerment. One of the best examples of this comes from the action framework developed by Chuck Salina, Suzann Girtz, and Joannie Eppinga. In their book called Powerless to Powerful or P2P (2016), coauthors Chuck Salina, Suzann Girtz, and Joanie Eppinga outline the conceptual and action frameworks of P2P and how it enables leaders to transform schools.

As explained in the Preface to Powerless to Powerful (2016), the system was first introduced in 2008 at a high school in Sunnyside, Washington. At the outset, the school's graduation rate stood at a concerning 49%. However, with the implementation of Powerless to Powerful principles and practices, the school underwent a remarkable transformation. Within four years, the graduation rate soared to an impressive 85%; by 2020, nearly 90% of students were successfully graduating (Salina et al., 2016).

They achieved these results because Powerless to Powerful's essence lies in its ability to elevate academic achievement by fostering a supportive environment that embraces social support, academic rigor, and a foundation of trust among students, teachers, counselors, administrators, and parents. It guides the PLC to adopt principles and support systems that foster collaboration, shared vision, and a culture of learning. Ultimately, this approach encompasses a set of beliefs and behaviors that empower education leaders to drive positive change in schools.

I am introducing you to this concept because P2P is a transformational systems process that leads to second-order change when led by a servant leader. It is a foundational approach with tremendous capacity, when applied with sincerity and consistency, to transform the educational landscape of an organization. As you'll see in greater detail in the next chapter, Powerless to Powerful initiates the continuous improvement cycle because it emphasizes the role of leadership and the value of a leader who empowers rather than transacts.

When the leadership is shared, that paves the way for the PLC to work together to evaluate opportunities for growth, set priorities, develop action plans, and determine monitoring systems in a way that uplifts everyone. It is not about the leader saying, "You're going to do this because I said so." The leader acknowledges that the organization has requirements to meet and says, "Let's look at the data, come up with a plan, and see if we make gains." The leader doesn't dictate *how* (unless processes are mandated) but supports team members to lead their own action research and share their results.

Whenever changes are applied with a focus on only one component, like systems or data, without nurturing relationships or sharing the collaborative action research, it risks becoming transactional in nature. Transactional leadership has one decision-maker and therefore does not promote growth or resilience.

WHAT DOES SUCCESS LOOK LIKE?

When transformational leaders are installed in a PLC, success looks like a community of educators working together to develop their strengths and expertise. For example, reading and math teachers are paired based on their strengths, and expert teachers rotate the students through different classes, sharing their knowledge and exploring learning with the students. This approach focuses on developing teachers' strengths, which leads to transformation in the children and is celebrated as the outcome of the learning organization.

The success of transformational leadership can be seen in the growth and development of each expert teacher, as well as in the overall success of the learners and the organization. In this kind of learning community, experts are identified based on their strengths and their ability to transform others, and they are evaluated on how well they use that success to serve students and families. Mutual respect is shown for each expert's contributions to the organization's overall success, and the community works together to ensure every student can succeed.

HOW DO YOU KNOW YOU'VE BECOME A TRANSFORMATIONAL LEADER?

You will know you have become a transformational leader when you start seeing transformation in your community, the people involved, and the idea of leadership itself. It is not just about achieving results but about how you achieve them. As a transformational leader, you lead by example and model the behaviors you want to see in others. You inspire others to reach their full potential and encourage them to develop their own leadership abilities. You create a shared vision and work collaboratively toward achieving it. You are always seeking opportunities to improve yourself and those around you. Most importantly, you are dedicated to serving the community's needs rather than just your own interests.

Transformational leadership is mentored; as the student becomes ready, the mentor arrives. Former US Ambassador to South Africa, Delano Lewis, speaks to this process of tapping by a mentor in *It All Begins with Self* (2016). To become a transformational leader, you start by looking at yourself and identifying your strengths and areas where you need support. Then, you can find mentors, guides, or training to help you improve in areas where you are not as strong. You also determine how to find the right people for your team who can contribute their unique strengths and skills to your shared vision. As you lead your team toward this vision, you focus on transforming the community, the people involved, and the idea of leadership itself. By being a role model, inspiring others, and always seeking to improve yourself and those around you, you can become a truly transformational leader.

RESILIENCE INSIGHTS

- Transformational leadership empowers individuals within an organization, promoting a sense of ownership and shared responsibility. This empowerment fosters resilience as team members become more engaged, motivated, and capable of overcoming challenges. The leader's focus on developing future leaders creates a culture of support, leading to increased adaptability and resilience.

- Transformational leaders guide their teams through this change by embracing continuous improvement cycles and a collaborative approach. Resilience is essential as individuals navigate uncertainties associated with cultural shifts and adapt to new ways of thinking and behaving.

4
CYCLES OF CONTINUOUS IMPROVEMENT

"Action research is a small idea. It involves examining data on one's work to help improve one's performance."

— *RICHARD D. SAGOR*

I know I have spent considerable time (two whole chapters!) on the type of leader you must be in order to effect change, but I need you to understand that servant leadership and transformational leadership is the foundation of the rest of this book. You cannot hope to succeed with the remainder of this guide unless you strive to embody the traits and mindset from the last two chapters. That is because the continuous improvement I keep referencing relies on leaders who can put the mission before themselves and create a culture of shared leadership.

In the last chapter, I touched on how transformational leadership gets the team moving in the same direction, beginning the continuous improvement cycle of change. In this chapter, I want to expand on this continuous improvement cycle and how it functions in a learning organization. By the end of this chapter, you will see why the last two were so important and how to begin this work for yourself. First, consider the following graphic from the *Powerless to Powerful Coaches' Handbook* (2019). It outlines the three elements that comprise the culture of learning.

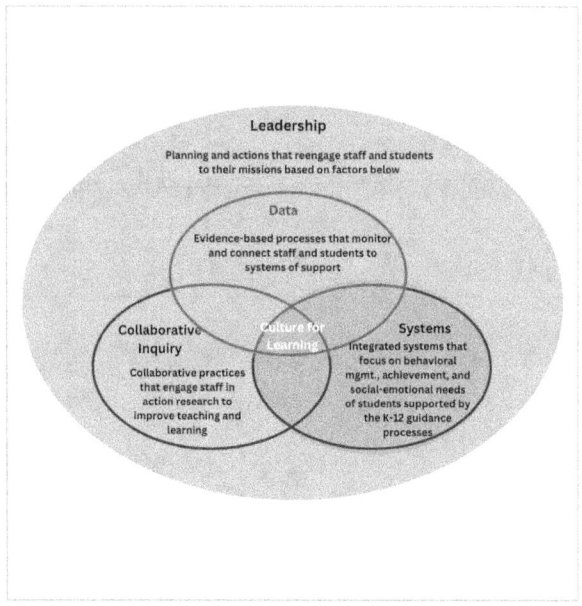

(Figure 2: School Improvement Action Framework from
Powerless to Powerful Coaches' Handbook. *Salina et. al,*
2019)

As you can see, transformational leadership undergirds this entire process.

WHAT ARE THE CYCLE AND ITS COMPONENTS?

This action framework is designed to guide work and initiatives toward achieving a specific goal. The three components of this continuous improvement cycle are data, collaborative inquiry, and systems.

Data:

Data forms the bedrock of the continuous improvement cycle, providing the necessary evidence to make informed decisions and identify areas for enhancement. When initiating the cycle, it is essential to carefully select relevant data points that align with the research questions at hand.

For example, let's say assessing the comprehension of English Language Learner (ELL) students for a specific piece of literature designated by your state standard. In this scenario, the chosen data points would revolve around the proximity of the students' scores to the age-appropriate standards. You could categorize them as standard, below standard, and exceeds standard. The ultimate goal is to identify areas for growth and then develop effective methodologies that support student learning and improvement. Therefore, having reliable data that accurately reflects progress becomes essential in measuring the attainment of set goals. (Note: The more specific your categories, the more valuable your data becomes, as discussed in great detail in Chapter 6.)

This data-driven approach empowers schools to drive meaningful change and ensure the success of their students. It enables leadership to remove guesswork to address the true needs of students and set priorities accurately. This makes it much easier to get buy-in as initiatives are aligned to something concrete. Finally, this approach makes it easier to build morale and momentum because educators are more capable of finding and addressing quick wins.

One thing to remember is that you may need three main types of data: qualitative, quantitative, and triangulated.

Qualitative data is descriptive data that cannot be measured numerically. It is collected through observation, interviews, and other methods that allow for collecting rich, detailed information. Qualitative data is often used to understand complex phenomena like human behavior or attitudes. Examples of qualitative data include written responses to open-ended survey questions, field notes from observations, and transcripts from interviews. Within qualitative data, there is a subset called heuristic data, which is a "story-based" historical development that shows impact over time.

Quantitative data is numerical data that can be measured and analyzed statistically. It is collected through methods such as surveys, tests, and experiments. Quantitative data is often used to measure the effectiveness of interventions or to compare groups. Examples of quantitative data include test scores, survey responses using Likert scales, and demographic information.

Triangulated data is a type of data that combines multiple sources or methods of data collection to increase the reliability and validity of the data. It involves using two or more different methods to study the same phenomenon, such as comparing survey responses with observations or interviews with document analysis. By triangulating data, you can check for consistency across different sources and methods. In the context of a learning organization, triangulated data can be useful to gain a comprehensive understanding of student performance, identify patterns and trends, and inform decision-making for continuous improvement. In this scenario, you would use both quantitative and qualitative data.

For instance, you may use grades, teacher observation, and student satisfaction surveys as your three data points. Grades would be quantitative, while teacher observation and student satisfaction surveys are qualitative. All three are important to ensuring student growth and achievement because they inform and guide differentiated (individualized) instruction and teacher match. When we're talking about students, this sort of approach is vital because you're not looking at a one-dimensional subject. Many factors (such as their social-emotional frame) impact others and add to or hinder the trajectory of each student's ultimate level of success.

All three data types - qualitative, quantitative, and triangulated - are important for making informed decisions and guiding improvement efforts for the entire organization. This is how you will begin to analyze systems for continuous improvement of the organization.

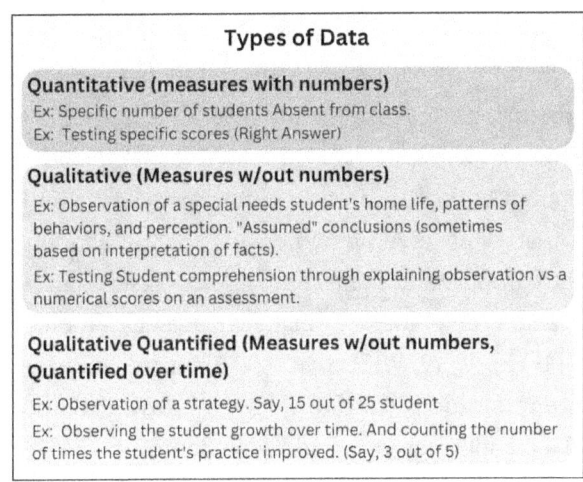

Types of Data

Quantitative (measures with numbers)
Ex: Specific number of students Absent from class.
Ex: Testing specific scores (Right Answer)

Qualitative (Measures w/out numbers)
Ex: Observation of a special needs student's home life, patterns of behaviors, and perception. "Assumed" conclusions (sometimes based on interpretation of facts).
Ex: Testing Student comprehension through explaining observation vs a numerical scores on an assessment.

Qualitative Quantified (Measures w/out numbers, Quantified over time)
Ex: Observation of a strategy. Say, 15 out of 25 student
Ex: Observing the student growth over time. And counting the number of times the student's practice improved. (Say, 3 out of 5)

(Figure 3: Examples of Different Data Types)

Collaborative Inquiry:

Collaborative inquiry is a process that involves teams of educators working together to investigate a particular issue, question, or problem. The process often begins by defining the problem or question and then collecting data to understand the issue better. This data may include student work samples, observation notes, or other data relevant to the issue being studied.

Once the data has been collected, the team engages in a process of analysis and interpretation to make sense of the data and identify patterns or trends. This analysis may involve using statistical analysis tools or other data analysis methods. The team may also use thinking maps or other graphic organizers to help them clarify their thinking and identify relationships between different aspects of the data.

Based on their analysis of the data, the team then develops and implements a plan of action designed to address the issue or problem they have identified. This action plan may involve trying out different instructional strategies, modifying the curriculum, or changing the learning environment. The team then continues to collect data and monitor progress over time to evaluate the effectiveness of their interventions and make further adjustments as needed.

Throughout the collaborative inquiry process, it is important to focus on student learning and ensure that all actions taken are designed to improve student outcomes. This requires ongoing reflection and a willingness to make changes based on new information and evidence. Effective collaborative inquiry requires strong communication skills, the ability to work effectively as a team, and a commitment to continuous improvement.

Systems:

In order to support the continuous improvement cycle, it is important to establish systems for monitoring research and sustaining positive outcomes. These systems should be designed to gather and analyze data and provide regular feedback to staff and stakeholders to make instructional decisions. It is also essential to have a process for updating these systems with the emergence of new data to ensure that they remain relevant and effective over time. By establishing strong systems for monitoring and sustaining improvement efforts, organizations can ensure that they are making progress toward their goals and continuously improving with time.

One example of a system within a learning organization or PLC is using pre- and post-assessments to monitor student progress and guide instructional decisions. Before instruction begins, teachers administer a pre-assessment to assess student knowledge and identify any areas where students may need additional support. Based on the pre-assessment results, teachers can adjust their instructional approach to better meet the needs of their students. After instruction is completed, teachers administer a post-assessment to evaluate student learning and determine the effectiveness of their instructional approach. The data from pre- and post-assessments can also be used to identify areas where additional support or enrichment may be necessary and to guide future instructional decisions. By using pre- and post-assessments as part of a larger system for monitoring student progress and guiding instruction, teachers and PLCs can continuously improve their practice and support student learning.

While we are talking about systems, I want to bring your attention to another model or framework: PITS. This stands for **people, ideas, things,** and **systems** and comes from the work of professor and researcher Richard Wolfe. He has devised a method for identifying solutions within a PLC and analyzing the components to design a plan of action as options A, B, and C. This allows for a PLC to plan for one approach. Then, if it doesn't work, they have a ready plan to adapt and apply a new approach at the moment based on data that has informed the PLC to take a quick turn in another direction. This might be a slight tweak that the previous option reveals as a more productive method for achieving more refined results.

PITS Model for Decision-Making
Developed by Richard Wolfe

	Option A	Option B	Option C
People	How many Teachers, Students, Support Adults		
Ideas	Matching the number of adults to the needs of the Students		
Things	Resources, Tools, Buses, Etc.		
Systems	Special Ed. Behavior Management, Office Management for attendance		

(Figure 4. PITS Model for Decision-Making and Problem-Solving)

The PITS model, represented in Figure 4, is a powerful decision-making framework that empowers school administrators to navigate complex challenges effectively. Let's delve into the key components of PITS, as depicted in the chart, and gain insights into how it supports decision-making and systems improvement in schools:

1. **People:** At the heart of the PITS model are the people. Administrators can personalize solutions and the relationship of the desired results by considering diverse perspectives, including teachers, students, support staff, and parents.

2. **Ideas:** Ideas are the foundational values that underpin each option being considered. By understanding the core principles driving these choices, administrators can ensure alignment with the school's overall goals and vision.

3. **Things:** Tangible resources and elements, such as the number of staff members, financial allocations, time availability, and necessary tools, play a crucial role in

decision-making. These practical considerations ensure the feasibility and effectiveness of chosen options.

4. **Systems:** Measuring the effectiveness of options A, B, and C is essential for continuous improvement. Robust data collection and analysis methods empower administrators to monitor progress, evaluate outcomes, and make data-driven adjustments.

School administrators can leverage the PITS model in various scenarios, such as during the budget process or when refining instructional methods. For instance, in budget planning, administrators can present different revisions (Option A, Option B, Option C) for managing busing. Seeking input from the parent community through focus groups, surveys, or committee meetings, leaders can gather feedback and make revisions that best serve the community's needs while working within budget constraints.

Likewise, we can apply this approach when we notice students struggling to grasp a particular concept using our current teaching method. For instance, it may occur with a reading curriculum that confuses students on specific vocabulary or concepts, especially in subjects like science or social studies. In response, we collaborate within a PLC to devise an alternative instructional approach that differs from the standard curriculum, aiming to achieve better results with our students. If this new approach proves effective, we implement it with the group of students it benefits. Additionally, we design option B for a specific subgroup and perhaps option C for another subgroup of special needs students, utilizing diverse methods such as auditory, visual, and kinesthetic techniques to impart the same concept.

Following this method will help leaders continue to improve systems that support student outcomes because it embraces a process of continuous improvement and data-driven revision. As a method of continuous improvement, strategies and modifications are based on factual information (data), but the options are designed and applied based on the PLC relationship with those affected. It becomes a respectful process of decision-making only by the PLC personalizing it to the people involved in the decision and those the decision will impact. This is where equity and inclusivity become extremely important. This often means collecting input from and communicating outcomes to the parents who don't speak English or the patrons/stakeholders with differing views (such as whether to wear masks or not to wear masks, when and where, mandatory vaccination, or alternative schooling).

Moreover, this approach fosters resilience within a PLC through its flexible and collaborative nature. As the options are applied with minor adjustments, a shared resolution emerges, mutually accepted by all parties involved. When decisions are reached collectively and supported by the PITS framework, the group can trust that all possible alternatives were considered, ensuring the best possible outcome for the majority. Additionally, options are provided for those who may choose not to accept the majority choice, ensuring inclusivity and equity within the decision-making process.

Furthermore, in the context of instruction, resilience is cultivated when instructors adapt their teaching methods to cater to different types of learners on a specific concept. By differentiating instruction to accommodate various learning styles and abilities, momentum builds, leading to increased academic achievements among students. This instructional approach, known as differentiation, prioritizes growth for all learners rather than solely targeting the majority, creating a resilient learning environment that empowers every student to succeed.

HOW DOES IT ALL FIT TOGETHER?

These three components—data, collaborative inquiry, and systems —fit together to create a cycle of continuous improvement within a learning organization or PLC. The cycle begins with the collection and analysis of data, which provides the evidence needed to identify areas for improvement. One thing that is not discussed as frequently is that you don't want to stop at just looking for problems. It is important and valuable to identify positive outliers (individuals who achieved above-average results).

Once data is collected, teams engage in a process of collaborative inquiry to investigate a particular issue, question, or problem or to identify ways to replicate outlier success. Based on their analysis of the data, the team develops and implements a plan of action designed to address the issue or problem they have identified. Finally, systems are established to monitor and sustain improvement efforts over time, which allows for ongoing reflection and refinement of the process.

When these elements are applied within a transformational leadership framework, it generates a culture for learning and long-term success. Remember that a transformational leader develops a culture of shared leadership and honors the talents each member contributes. It is vital to invite everyone to participate in creating a path forward, building a culture of collaboration and trust. When teams can work together effectively, leveraging the strengths of each team member and working through challenges and setbacks, a culture of continuous improvement begins to emerge, creating the necessary resilience to keep moving toward increased outcomes.

TQM & LITTLE MOUNTAIN

Much of what we're talking about when it comes to collaborative inquiry comes from Richard Sagor, who has pioneered the concept of "collaborative action research" and its application in various settings, including education and leadership. It became popularly known as TQM in leadership. In his book *Guiding School Improvement With Action Research* (2000), Sagor redefined and applied this process in the classroom, specifically focusing on instructional practice in areas such as reading and math. In Salina et. al's P2P coaching guide (2019), this approach can be particularly powerful in promoting a culture of continuous improvement, involving staff in identifying problems, devising solutions, testing them, and refining instructional practices to achieve better student outcomes.

Here is a breakdown of how the process works using English reading and writing as an example: If a leader or teacher notices a decrease in comprehension or vocabulary scores on a reading test at a particular grade level (using data), they would define a process to implement an intervention and then test its effectiveness in improving student outcomes. (Inquiry.) The instructional process would then be refined based on the results to create greater growth. The teacher would measure the newly applied process and assess if further improvements can be made to achieve even greater student growth. (Systems.)

Let's say the focus is on vocabulary. The teacher might test a strategy to enhance students' understanding of math-related words, such as math practices. This testing and refinement process would typically take place over a period of 30 to 45 days, followed by an assessment of improvement. Based on the results, instructional practices and student-specific learning strategies would be adjusted or improved accordingly.

Altogether, the continuous improvement process involves

identifying areas for improvement, implementing interventions, testing their effectiveness, and refining instructional practices based on the results. By observing and evaluating both the growth opportunities and the *positive outliers*, this iterative process allows for ongoing refinement in educational practices, leading to enhanced student outcomes.

Let me share a story illustrating how this approach can be applied within an organization. Years ago, I was hired as the principal of Little Mountain Elementary, a brand-new school in Mount Vernon, Washington. The school was set to be cutting-edge, with a generous grant of $300,000 from Microsoft through Western Washington University for teacher training and technological equipment. The staff was provided with new computers, and we had an HP lab for learning Microsoft software to support student learning, setting the stage for utilizing data as a key component of our improvement process. This was a part of the Home Education and Ready Teacher (H.E.A.R.T.) project in 1997 (Clauson and Myhre, 2000).

To effectively use the technology resources, I organized a committee of staff members into a tech team to engage in collaborative inquiry. Together, we explored how technology could enhance literacy skills and promote inclusivity in our diverse student population at Little Mountain Elementary. We identified areas such as science, weather, and friendship where technology could be integrated into the curriculum to enhance literacy.

This collaborative inquiry led to the implementation of various strategies, including using mind maps, such as circle maps and double bubble maps, to promote critical thinking and writing skills. For example, students used Venn diagrams to compare and contrast ideas related to friendship, highlighting similarities and differences. This approach was especially important for our bilingual community, which had a significant population of English Language Learner Spanish-speaking students. We collected and analyzed data, in the form of student work and engagement, to inform the effectiveness of these strategies in improving literacy outcomes.

We also recognized the importance of involving parents in our improvement process. We organized parent nights and provided resources such as Sony PlayStation and CDs with stories to promote English language development at home. Teachers conducted home visits to gather data on student reading progress at home and their participation in school events. This data, along with attendance data and student feedback, helped inform the effectiveness of the strategies in involving parents as partners in improving literacy.

Finally, we focused on systems to support continuous improvement. We put systems in place to ensure that technology resources were effectively utilized and staff and parents were engaged in the collaborative inquiry process. We created a welcoming environment where all students felt valued and included, addressing the diverse needs of our student population.

As a result of this comprehensive approach, we observed positive outcomes, including increased attendance, engagement, and academic growth. Our school community came together holistically, with students, parents, and staff collaborating to promote literacy skills and inclusivity. A leadership model similar to the Powerless to Powerful model (which emerged in 2016) , with its emphasis on data, collaborative inquiry, and systems, was instrumental in guiding our work at Little Mountain Elementary. Within three years, we became an outlier school in student written literacy with English when our students represented a 60% English Language Learners (ELL) in Spanish with impressive test scores.

THE RESILIENCE FACTOR

When you read the previous section, it may sound like the process went smoothly. However, if you know anything about education or working in a new building, you will understand that work like this is seldom without its challenges. To make this continuous improvement process work, you need a way to meet all of the challenges and build resilience.

To put this in perspective, I would like you to imagine the pressure of being days from opening day (when students would be in the building) and not having enough seats. Imagine there being no textbooks and the fire safety sprinkler system turning on during the middle of class time. Imagine trying to prepare an educational environment on an active construction site and having no school telephone for two weeks after opening. Parents trying to reach educators and administrators had no consistent way of connecting with us—which was only exacerbated by the fact that 60% of students had Spanish-speaking families. Imagine having 100 more students than the facility's opening capacity and having to orchestrate the addition of portables.

All of these were examples of the day-to-day challenges we faced on location. Though the future looked bright with the groundbreaking technology, the present-day on the ground was unappealing, to say the least. As a leader, I had to ask myself, "How do I hold the vision of what this place could truly be? How do I keep the team together?" The most important thing to remember was that it was not just me. We were a team of leaders working together to bring this vision to fruition.

What proved the most trying was actually a clash of directives or vision. At Little Mountain, we were building a site-based transformational culture. While we were facing the aforementioned struggles to be operational for students, there were times when the district's priorities did not completely align with our program needs. For example, while we were wondering where our text-books were, having parent volunteers build desks, and figuring out how to get the toilets to flush properly (imagine that if you can), they were wondering about how we would police students skateboarding on the new campus.

All of these things were important, but this misalignment caused a lack of trust among the school staff as they wondered if they would ever get what they needed to do the jobs they had signed up for. These educators believed in the vision and were passionate about collaborating to create this transformational culture on-site. Yet, they were met with a transactional, top-down direction that seemed removed from the immediate crisis. In this scenario, many voices needed to be heard and responded to—staff, the district, the students, and the families. Initially, it seemed like we were all in competition when we should have been collabo-rating and recognizing that we were on the same team.

In order to stay the course, we at the school *all* had to double down on our belief in this transformational process. Staff members became exceptional at mining for data to find areas that *could* be acted on and improved for student achievement and support despite not having all of the necessary systems. There came a point where this team's understanding blossomed, and we started seeing more significant gains. But before that, we had to commit to the improvement cycle and shared ownership.

This opened the door to one of the most valuable resilience factors: compounding momentum. The situation described above was demoralizing, so doubling down on the improvement cycle meant not chasing behind a constant list of problems but finding opportunities for greater gains. When we completed an inquiry and testing process and began looking at the data, we made sure to look for the positive outliers, the ones who exceeded expecta-tions. We investigated what might have caused that level of performance and developed new tests to see if those results could be replicated.

By shifting focus from problems to wins, we built curiosity. Success feels good, so exploring ways to expand what was working was rewarding instead of only looking at what needed fixing. This provided the morale to keep running the process until we had become an outlier school in English writing within the district in just under three years.

FINAL THOUGHT

Long-term success and greater gains in student outcomes hinge on how well leaders in a PLC start and keep this continuous improvement cycle rolling. While the cycle propels itself with the aforementioned components, it is underpinned by the effectiveness of the leadership. When you have a transformational leader, you can run the process. When you run the process, you empower your team and stakeholders to develop strategies that work for everyone involved. In the upcoming chapter, we will shift our focus to the concept of creative tension to see how it can foster innovation and speed up the rate of change within your organization.

RESILIENCE INSIGHTS

- The three interconnected components of the continuous improvement cycle embed resilience within a learning organization by building a data-driven, collaboratively owned, outcome-focused scaffolding for operating. Once the wheel starts to turn, you simply move through the phases.

- Initiating the continuous improvement process requires a transformational leader who embraces resilience to keep steering the ship. Obstacles such as lack of resources, misaligned priorities, and immediate operational issues can be demoralizing, and the leader has to model and reinforce resilience for the team.
- Resilience is enhanced through the shift from a problem-focused to a win-focused approach. As the team concentrates on positive outliers and explores their success factors, this perspective shift fosters curiosity and morale, leading to increased motivation and commitment to the continuous improvement cycle. Building on successes creates compounding momentum that fuels stable and consistent growth.

5
CREATIVE TENSION

"The gap between vision and current reality is also a source of energy. If there were no gap, there would be no need for any action to move toward the vision. We call this gap creative tension."

— PETER SENGE

To begin this chapter, I want to give you a somewhat humorous image to hold onto. Imagine you have a jar with a handful of jumping beans. If you have never heard of these, they are harvested from the shrub that is native to Mexico. These seed pods are often brown in color, about the size of a pea, and contain a small larva of a peculiar moth species. The larva's movements make the beans wiggle and "jump." For this illustration, I want you to imagine them in a little more animated fashion.

As you watch the beans in the jar, you observe that most of them tend to jump to a height of about two-thirds of the way up the jar. Most of the remaining beans only make it halfway, but a small number consistently jump completely out of the jar. (Astounding!) As you put the lid on the jar, you begin to wonder why they jump at different heights. What factors play into how high a bean can jump?

Once the lid is on, you notice a change. Something about the pressure has agitated the beans, and they all seem to jump a bit higher. Some of the low jumpers are now jumping above the halfway line, and many of the average beans have started crashing into the underside of the lid. After seeing these gains, another question comes to mind: What would it take to get the beans to pop the lid off?

This metaphor illustrates the basic methodology of *creative tension*. In the pursuit of continuous improvement within our learning organizations, leaders strive to achieve better outcomes, enhance performance, and drive positive outcomes for student learning. As discussed in the previous chapter, collaborative action research has proven to be a powerful mechanism for understanding complex problems and fostering collective efforts toward improvement. In this chapter, we will delve into the concept of creative tension to understand how it can amplify the continuous improvement cycle and unlock new possibilities for innovation and positive outliers.

WHAT IS CREATIVE TENSION?

Creative Tension is a dynamic concept in the fields of personal and organizational change, popularized by Robert Fritz and Peter Senge in their respective books, *The Path of Least Resistance* (Fritz, 1989) and *The Fifth Discipline: The Art and Practice of the Learning Organization* (Senge, 1990). According to Fritz, Creative Tension is a natural force that propels individuals toward change and innovation. It creates a gap between their current reality and their desired outcome, stimulating creativity, problem-solving, and action taking. Similarly, Senge sees creative tension as a key element of Personal Mastery, one of the disciplines of organizational learning, where a clear and compelling vision of the future creates a gap or tension with the current reality, motivating individuals to take action, learn from feedback, and continuously improve.

I would like to add that creative tension is about the boundaries or bookends that you put on a system. Think back to our jar of jumping beans. This could symbolize student achievement in school, with the height jumped representing test scores. The jar acts as a metaphorical container, and putting the lid on it symbolizes applying pressure to change results. Observing that the beans jump to different heights, with positive and negative outliers, the desired outcome would be to increase the number of positive outliers. This approach can be applied in schools and learning organizations using the core components of the continuous improvement cycle: data, collaborative inquiry, and systems.

Let's take, for example, the head of a high school English department who is passionate about creative writing and wants to introduce the concept of creative essays to help students think more creatively in their writing. To apply the concept of creative tension, the first step would be to create a clear and compelling vision of the desired outcome, imagining a future where students are able to produce engaging and innovative essays that showcase their creativity and critical thinking skills.

Next, data would be gathered on the current state of high school essays through pre-assessment assignments to establish a baseline for comparison and monitoring improvement. Gaps between the existing approach and the desired outcome would be identified, which could involve reviewing past student essays, examining the curriculum and teaching methods, and seeking feedback from students and colleagues.

Once the gaps are identified, the concept of creative tension would come into play during the collaborative inquiry phase, where members of the PLC work collaboratively to design experiments, share strategies, and discuss progress, also known as collaborative action research. Creative tension would be applied by affixing a clear timeline, such as 45 or 90 days, within which the team would work toward getting students to think and write more creatively. A shorter time frame would create higher pressure in the container, stimulating creativity, problem-solving, and action-taking due to the sense of urgency. The shorter timeline would also speed up the collection of new data to determine the effectiveness of the methodology.

Instead of assessing at the beginning and end of the year, the team would assess quarterly and expect gains. After the first quarter, new data on the teaching strategies and their impact on producing positive outliers would be collected. If the desired results are not achieved, interventions could be applied in the next round, and if successful, the team could double down on what worked to test replicability. Feedback loops would be established for monitoring progress as changes are implemented.

It's important to note that this approach to creative tension does not rely on the leader designing the strategy and imposing it on the team, which would be transactional. Instead, it follows a transformational process that involves the leader letting team members share in the development and implementation of ideas, acknowledging their creative dignity. The goal is to generate more ideas and test them faster to expedite the rate of change.

IT'S NOT ABOUT "FIXING"

When you approach continuous improvement with the right mindset and apply creative tension, you must remember that it's not about fixing problems but rather about identifying where you want to be and where you currently stand in the data analysis process. The tension lies in determining whether it's possible to reach your goal within a given timeframe and keeping the boundaries tight to shorten the timeline.

If your mindset is solely focused on fixing something, it can lead to a negative outlook where something is perceived as being wrong, and you risk driving your team into a loop of chasing problems and never making any gains. However, when you approach the situation with the correct mindset, you actively seek a solution and create a process to achieve a desired outcome in a specific timeframe.

It's important to look at both ends of the spectrum. For instance, if you want to raise the test scores of your school as a whole, your "low-hanging fruit" might be students who are just below the threshold of meeting standards. In this scenario, you would target efforts around that group to get them over the line. Continuous improvement begins when you then take those results and look for those who outperformed. Then you investigate whether those results can be replicated and expanded to make compounding gains across the spectrum over time. This approach is akin to building a tour guide, replicating the existing good processes, and building upon positive outcomes. By focusing on replicating success and making improvements, you are expanding the potential for gains and aiming to achieve results in a shorter time frame.

BEYOND THE CLASSROOM: CHALLENGING STRUCTURES

Transforming systems through this process requires a transformational leader who is willing to get into good trouble as they put pressure on systems. One such leader who exemplified this type of approach was Dr. Martin Luther King Jr., a prominent civil rights leader who utilized creative tension as a strategy to bring about social transformation. While creative tension is often associated with school improvement or organizational change, Dr. King's approach went beyond that, using tension to apply pressure to systems that needed rapid growth and catalyzing creative problem-solving. Drawing on various tactics and strategies, Dr. King effectively employed creative tension to challenge existing systems of discrimination and inequality during the Civil Rights Movement, leaving a lasting legacy as a transformational leader who used friction strategically for positive change in society.

As a transformational leader, Dr. King's approach was rooted in clearly defining the end game, which was the vision of equal opportunity for all. He strategically implemented multiple systems and interventions simultaneously to challenge the existing discriminatory practices, organizing impactful events such as sit-ins at lunch counters, marches across bridges, and demonstrations to protest against segregation and inequality. In addition, he drew attention to the unfair treatment of garbage collectors and voting rights issues. These actions intentionally created tension by disrupting the status quo and challenging the existing systems that perpetuated discrimination and inequality, serving as a powerful catalyst for social change.

King's use of creative tension was not limited to confrontation and conflict; he also employed nonviolent methods such as civil disobedience, peaceful protests, and civil rights activism. He drew inspiration from the teachings of Mahatma Gandhi, who also used similar tactics to challenge British colonial rule in India. King believed that nonviolent resistance could effectively bring about social change by appealing to the moral conscience of society and creating a sense of moral authority.

Despite encountering significant resistance and opposition, King understood that awareness of the issues was crucial for social change. The tension caused by King's interventions created discomfort and tension in society, but it also served as a catalyst for change. He effectively used the media to bring attention to the injustices and created opportunities for people to witness the discrimination firsthand. It forced people to confront the reality of discrimination and inequality and spurred conversations and debates about the need for social reform. The creative use of tension by King and his supporters created a sense of urgency and motivation among people to demand change and helped to galvanize public support and build momentum for the Civil Rights Movement.

King's approach was not without challenges and setbacks, but he persisted. He understood that change requires effort, perseverance, and resilience. He constantly analyzed the effectiveness of his interventions and adjusted his strategies based on the results. He was willing to take risks and push boundaries to achieve his goal of equal opportunity for all, and that is the point of creative tension—to create enough pressure to spur faster innovation.

You just have to remember that not all innovation is necessary or suitable for the community you serve. If you work in a diverse community, you must be aware of their priorities. In my own experience opening schools in the Middle East, for example, I learned that embracing culturally relevant approaches was crucial to success. I worked with a team to implement American-style education, but we quickly realized that we couldn't simply impose our Western education model without considering the local culture and stakeholders. This realization led us to adopt a culturally sensitive approach that honored the values, beliefs, and traditions of the Middle Eastern community.

One aspect of this approach was using culturally relevant literature in our curriculum. We carefully selected books that were relatable and appropriate for the Middle Eastern context, avoiding topics such as dancing, dogs, pigs, or Israel, which may not be suitable. Instead, we chose stories involving characters and settings familiar to the students, such as Arabian Nights, which resonated with Middle Eastern culture.

This approach of using culturally relevant literature in education raised an important question about the ongoing debate on book bans and cultural appropriateness in the United States. It made us reflect on whether education should be about changing culture or how we approach education. Creative Tension and continuous improvement require a nuanced approach that respects the cultural context and stakeholders involved. It is not just about fixing things but rather aligning with the needs, values, and beliefs of the communities being served. By embracing culturally relevant approaches, we can ensure that our projects are inclusive, respectful, and truly beneficial to all stakeholders involved.

STAYING THE COURSE

Dr. King's example brings us back to the topic at the heart of this book: resilience. In the previous chapters, resilience took the form of creating depth and strength within the organization. As a transformational leader, your work is to create more leaders behind you, right? That is one type of resilience, but it is not easy being a transformational leader in a transactional, hierarchical society.

At times, it can feel like you may not be making big enough gains. At times it may feel like you have too much resistance and combativeness. (Though Dr. King was a great leader, he was a martyr in the end, and we don't want that for you!) So the question is, how do you stay the course and commit to the cycle of continuous improvement?

The first thing I want you to hold onto is derived from an old Quaker quote that says:

"I shall pass this way but once; any good that I can do or any kindness I can show to any human being; let me do it now. Let me not defer or neglect it, for I shall not pass this way again."

—Stephen Grellet

In life, we are like pilgrims on our own journeys. We do not know how long we will be in any place. When I went to work in the Middle East, I had not expected to go. Nor had I expected to have to leave for surgery when I did. Nor did I know I would get to go back. When you're living as a servant leader, trying to make the world better through your work, you are on a pilgrimage, and like the speaker of this quote, you can only do good while you are in a space.

To me, this has always meant leaving a place better than I found it. Imagine you're firing a slingshot. You must first pull the elastic bands way back and put them under intense pressure in order for them to go as far forward as possible. Once you release it, it won't stay as far forward as it went, but it won't come as far back as it was. It will settle somewhere new.

Working as a transformational leader using the concept of creative tension is sort of like that. When you take over, you do it with the mindset of propelling the organization as far as possible while you're there and promoting a culture and systems that allow them to sustain momentum after you leave. You use the principles you've learned to build up leaders, instill a shared vision, and foster collaboration. You use creative tension to find opportunities for growth and keep building on that for as long as you can.

Then, when you face competing interests, like at Little Mountain and so many other communities, and when you face the individuals and groups who oppose the innovation you're working to bring for the good of the students you serve, you will be armed. You'll be armed with the knowledge that you don't need to do the work alone, nor do you need to martyr yourself. You will be able to recognize how far you can take an organization and then allow someone else to take the reins. This will enable you to save energy to go on serving in spaces where you can do the most good.

As I close this chapter, I want to leave you with just one takeaway: creative tension is not about conflict; it's about collaboration, promoting creative dignity within the organization, and using a timeline or "bookends" to make the most gains in the shortest amount of time. That is how you move the needle once you've established priorities *with* your team. This is how you begin the cycle so that it can sustain itself with or without you.

RESILIENCE INSIGHTS

- Creative Tension uses "bookends" (specific timeframes) in hopes of encouraging innovative strategies for bridging the gap between the present and desired states. This makes it possible to collect data and evaluate solutions more quickly to start finding positive outliers and, in turn, generates excitement and curiosity—a necessary component of a resilient organization.
- A transformational leader must foster and protect resilience by keeping one goal in mind: propelling the organization as far forward as possible within the time they have to leave it in better shape than when they arrived. This mindset keeps one's focus on building depth and strength within the team so that they take ownership of the process, take pride in the results, and desire to keep it going.

6

FOCUSED VS. DIFFUSED LIGHT

"If a man does not keep pace with his companions, perhaps it is because he hears a different drummer. Let him step to the music which he hears, however measured or far away."

— *HENRY DAVID THOREAU*

I magine you're standing outside at night, and it's dark. You want to point to something specific that is far away. You could use a flashlight, but you notice that it only illuminates what's up close, and the light isn't focused, so it illuminates a wide range. So instead, you pull out a laser pointer. The light from the laser travels much farther and is precisely focused exactly where you want it to be.

In the same way, imagine that you're a surgeon, and you need to make an incision. Consider the difference between using a flashlight and a laser. A flashlight provides light, but its broad beam makes it difficult to be precise. A laser, on the other hand, can be finely tuned to make precise incisions and operate on specific areas with accuracy and minimal damage to surrounding tissues.

The difference between using a flashlight and a laser is focused versus diffused light. Focus brings intensity, clarity, precision, and power. And it's this focus that we need to bring to education and transformational leadership. In education, being laser-focused means honing in on specific areas of need and designing targeted interventions to achieve specific goals. By doing so, educators can monitor progress, measure outcomes, and make data-informed decisions that lead to continuous improvement.

In the previous chapter, we discussed the concept of creative tension and using it to find outliers. We discussed how by identifying subscores and subgroups and focusing on specific them, educators can raise their scores and ultimately raise the scores of the whole class. In this chapter, we'll dive deeper into the idea of being laser-focused. We'll explore what it means to be intentional and targeted in our efforts and how we can use data to identify areas of improvement. By staying laser-focused on our goals, we can ensure that our efforts are effective and equitable and that we're making a real difference in the lives of our students.

WHAT DOES LASER-FOCUS LOOK LIKE IN EDUCATION?

Being laser-focused in education means being intentional and targeted in our efforts to achieve specific goals. It involves using data to identify areas of highest needs as well as positive outliers. This is done by identifying subscores of students rather than attempting to improve all students at once. By taking this approach, educators can make data-informed decisions that lead to continuous improvement through collaborative action research. To give you a clearer picture of what this looks like, I will start by breaking down subgroups.

WHAT ARE SUBSCORES?

Subscores are sets of data points that help educators identify subgroups of students who exhibit similar performance patterns but fall within different ranges. These subgroups can encompass students who perform above the standard, at the standard, just below the standard, or well below the standard. Each subgroup represents a distinct set of learners with specific learning needs or characteristics. By identifying these subgroups, educators can delve deeper into the reasons behind their varying performance levels and develop targeted teaching strategies to improve their skills and thereby improve their score. The goal is to address the unique needs of each subgroup rather than assuming a one-size-fits-all approach.

Recognizing subgroups goes beyond solely identifying under-performing students; it involves understanding the diverse needs of students within a larger group to implement more effective teaching strategies. Even students who perform well above the standard are considered positive outliers, and it is crucial to explore the methods and approaches that contribute to their exceptional success. By studying these high-performing subgroups, educators can uncover effective practices that can be replicated and applied to other students.

LASER-FOCUS IN PRACTICE

As a leader of education, I have witnessed firsthand the incredible impact of laser-focus in transforming student learning outcomes. Throughout my career, I have supported teams who utilized specific strategies and approaches to address the unique needs of subgroups of students. In this chapter, I will share with you some of my experiences and insights, highlighting the power of targeted teaching strategies.

One area where laser-focus has proved immensely beneficial is in the realm of reading literacy. I have seen remarkable results when education teams (PLCs) have employed strategies that specifically target subcategories such as storytelling, story structure, and comprehension. At Little Mountain, for instance, we implemented strategies to build vocabulary for ELL children. By tailoring our approaches to the needs of these learners, we were able to witness significant improvements in their reading abilities.

This laser-focused approach was not limited to Little Mountain alone. I have witnessed and led the implementation of similar strategies at Lewis and Clark High School, where I taught English Language Learner students. I also had the privilege of coaching first-grade teachers in Bahrain, working with children who spoke Arabic as their first language. In both instances, the emphasis was on enhancing language proficiency, vocabulary growth, and writing skills in the English language.

Now, let me provide you with a concrete example of how laser-focus translates into practice. Picture yourself as an English instructor to help students create better outlines. You have a diverse group of students, some of whom have never been introduced to the concept of outlining. To address this, you could take a diffused approach and teach the concept to the entire class, hoping that it will resonate with each student. However, this unfocused approach may lead to mixed results, as some students may grasp the concept while others remain perplexed.

Instead, by embracing laser-focus, you can tailor your teaching strategies to the specific needs of each subgroup. For instance, if a group of students is struggling with the concept of outlining, you can employ a targeted approach. One effective strategy I have used with young children is providing them with three-by-five index cards. Each card represents a section of the outline. For example, animals would be the topic, and the sub-topics would include items such as features, habitat, reproduction, and unique facts. By engaging them in hands-on activities, where they find facts in books and cite them on the cards, students learn the process of outlining and develop their research and organizational skills.

But what about the students who grasp the concept quickly? In this case, I believe in fostering a collaborative learning environment. By allowing these students to become leaders within their respective subgroups, they can assist their peers who are still struggling. This peer-to-peer support not only helps those who need additional guidance but also strengthens the understanding of the concept for the leaders themselves.

It is important to note that laser-focus goes beyond just instructional strategies. It also involves monitoring student progress, identifying areas of improvement, and making necessary adjustments. This ongoing assessment allows educators to address specific learning gaps, provide timely interventions, and ensure that every student has the opportunity to thrive.

Educators can create a classroom environment that nurtures individual growth and maximizes student potential by prioritizing subcategories and using laser-focus. It enables us to move away from diffused education, where we throw various instructional approaches without a clear plan or monitoring system. Instead, we adopt a targeted and purposeful approach that empowers students to reach their full potential.

DEVELOPING TARGETED STRATEGIES

Developing targeted strategies is crucial in addressing the unique needs of students and fostering their academic growth. Educators can create a tailored approach that maximizes student learning outcomes by providing individualized instruction, targeted interventions, and differentiated learning experiences. (Clauson &

Loshbaugh 1988). The question is, how do you employ this in classrooms?

Once subgroups are identified, educators can employ peer grouping to gain deeper insights into the specific needs of each subgroup. By dividing the class into peer groups, educators can allocate focused attention to different areas of instruction based on the subscores derived from assessment data. During dedicated class time, educators can rotate between each group, engaging in discussions and asking targeted questions to investigate why students in each subgroup may have struggled with their respective concepts.

This interactive dialogue allows educators to gather valuable information about students' learning experiences, challenges, and misconceptions. With this knowledge in hand, educators can then develop targeted strategies that address the specific needs of each subgroup. By combining the power of peer grouping and investigative discussions, educators can refine their instructional approaches and design interventions that have the potential to make a meaningful impact on student learning and achievement.

Collaboration plays a crucial role in harnessing educators' collective wisdom and experience. This collaborative approach involves engaging teachers, administrators, and other stakeholders in meaningful discussions and joint efforts to improve student learning outcomes.

Within this collaborative framework, teachers take the lead in conducting research within their own classrooms. They implement targeted strategies, collect data on their effectiveness, and analyze the results. By empowering teachers to lead the research, the focus remains on the real-world experiences and insights of those working directly with the students.

Leaders have a crucial role in facilitating collaborative discussions and creating a supportive environment where educators can come together to share their experiences, discuss student data, and explore possible interventions. The collaborative dialogue allows educators to learn from one another, identify patterns and trends, and brainstorm effective strategies to address the specific needs of subgroups.

To make the most of assessment data, leaders can organize teams for thorough analysis and interpretation. These teams can consist of educators from various disciplines, allowing for a comprehensive examination of student performance across different subject areas. The insights gained from these analyses can inform the development of targeted strategies that address common challenges subgroups face.

Additionally, leaders play a pivotal role in removing barriers hindering educators' ability to effectively engage in collaborative action research. By providing necessary resources, such as time for collaboration, access to data analysis tools, and professional development opportunities, leaders create an environment conducive to collaborative growth and innovation.

Collaboration extends beyond individual classrooms or departments. It involves sharing best practices and experiences across the school or district. Leaders can facilitate opportunities for educators to present their successful strategies, discuss their implementation, and provide support and guidance to their peers. This collective sharing of knowledge fosters a culture of continuous improvement and ensures that effective strategies are disseminated and replicated.

By embracing a collaborative approach, educators and leaders work together to develop targeted strategies that leverage the collective expertise of the teaching staff. This collaborative action research enables educators to refine their instructional practices, identify effective interventions, and continuously enhance the learning experiences for all students.

MEASURING SUCCESS

Measuring the success of specific strategies is a vital task for PLCs, and it involves the continuous monitoring and evaluation of student progress over time. This involves setting clear and measurable goals for each targeted strategy and collecting relevant data to assess effectiveness. Data collection includes quantitative measures such as assessments and test scores and qualitative data that captures students' learning experiences and growth.

By analyzing the data, PLCs can identify trends, patterns, and positive outliers—students who have achieved exceptional results. Studying these outliers helps uncover the factors that contribute to their success. PLCs also compare current data with baseline measurements to assess growth and progress. This comprehensive analysis allows them to evaluate strategy effectiveness and make informed decisions for improvement.

Reflective discussions and collaborative analysis are crucial for PLCs to identify the strengths and weaknesses of their strategies. This process helps them determine areas for further development and refine instructional approaches, interventions, and support mechanisms. Through consistent measurement and monitoring of student progress, PLCs can make evidence-based decisions, adapt practices, and improve learning outcomes.

Measuring success goes beyond data analysis. Celebrating the achievements and growth of students and subgroups is an integral part of the process. Recognizing their progress through positive reinforcement and motivation creates a culture of continuous improvement within PLCs. This celebration of success inspires educators and reinforces the commitment to striving for even greater outcomes.

In summary, PLCs leverage ongoing data analysis, collaborative reflection, and evidence-based decision-making to measure the success of specific strategies. This approach allows them to continuously improve practices, enhance student learning experiences, and achieve desired educational outcomes.

THE RISKS OF NOT BEING FOCUSED

Now that you understand the benefit of this laser-focused approach, I want to help you see what is at stake by not implementing this strategy. In short, when we as leaders of education fail to prioritize focused interventions, several challenges can arise, hindering student progress and impeding overall outcomes.

One of the primary risks is the potential waste of valuable time and resources. Without laser-focus instructional time may be dispersed across various areas, leading to a lack of depth and mastery in any specific skill or concept. Students may receive fragmented instruction, which can result in confusion, gaps in knowledge, and limited growth. In the absence of targeted interventions, students can easily get lost in the educational journey, unable to access the support and guidance they need to thrive.

Another risk is the accumulation of gaps in learning. When instruction lacks direction and a solid foundation, students may struggle to build upon previous knowledge and skills. Unaddressed gaps can compound over time, leading to significant challenges in later years. Without a laser-focused approach, educators may find themselves in a constant cycle of trying to cover missed content, leaving little room for advanced learning and growth.

On the other hand, when laser-focus is applied, gains in student achievement can be compounded. By targeting specific subgroups and implementing tailored strategies, educators can address individual needs and provide the necessary support for growth. This intentional approach fosters a solid foundation of knowledge and skills, enabling students to progress steadily and confidently. With each small gain, students gain momentum, building their self-confidence and motivation for continued learning.

THE ROLE OF RESILIENCE IN LASER-FOCUS

Resilience plays a vital role in the implementation of laser-focused strategies. It is a quality that is cultivated not only in students but also in instructors and educational leaders. Through the laser-focused approach, both students and educators develop resilience and adaptability, enabling them to overcome challenges and achieve exceptional outcomes.

The laser-focused approach nurtures resilience for students by providing tailored support and interventions that address their specific needs. They experience personalized learning experiences that empower them to overcome barriers, build their strengths, and reach their full potential. As students see their progress and witness their own growth, they become more resilient learners, equipped with the confidence and determination to face future academic challenges.

Educators, too, develop resilience through the laser-focused approach. By continuously monitoring student progress, analyzing data, and adjusting instructional strategies, educators become more adaptable in meeting the diverse needs of their students. They learn to identify areas for improvement, modify teaching methods, and seek out innovative approaches to enhance student outcomes. The resilience of educators translates into a dynamic and responsive learning environment that supports the success of all students. One of the things about becoming resilient is developing the concept and awareness of themselves as leaders. They are the ones who set the parameters and goals, conduct research, review data, and guide the improvement cycle.

The impact of laser-focus and resilience extends beyond the classroom walls. Principals and educational leaders witness the growth and collaboration within the school community, igniting their excitement and belief in the power of a laser-focused approach. This enthusiasm spreads to leaders in central offices, who begin to ask supportive questions and provide the necessary resources and guidance. As the system becomes more resilient, partnerships are formed, and the community's collective efforts come into play. Parents and the broader community witness the success of the individualized learning approach, inspiring them and fostering a sense of shared responsibility for educational excellence. Laser-focus and intentional support create empowered leaders and instruction helping people grow.

Altogether, the risks of not being laser-focused in education are evident. Without targeted strategies, valuable time and resources can be wasted, students may get lost, and gaps in learning may accumulate. However, the educational landscape transforms when resilience is embraced and a laser-focused approach is adopted. Students develop resilience, educators become more adaptable, and a sense of excitement and collaboration permeates the learning community.

RESILIENCE INSIGHTS

- Implementing a laser-focused approach in education nurtures resilience in both students and educators. Tailored support and interventions foster students' confidence and determination to overcome challenges, while educators' adaptability in monitoring progress and adjusting strategies enhances the learning environment's responsiveness.

- Resilience and laser-focus extend beyond the classroom, inspiring school communities, educational leaders, parents, and the broader community. A sense of shared responsibility for educational excellence emerges, driven by the success of the individualized learning approach and its impact on student outcomes.

7
PARTNERSHIPS

"If you want to go fast, go alone. If you want to go far, go together."

— *ATTRIBUTED TO AN AFRICAN PROVERB*

When I was little, my parents owned a fishing resort by a calm and serene lake. It was a place where people came to relax and enjoy the simple pleasure of casting their fishing lines into the water. And there, in that peaceful haven, I met a woman who would forever change how I saw myself.

Missy was a beautiful African American woman with a confident and graceful presence that reminds me of Michelle Obama today. My parents became good friends with her and her husband, and I spent a lot of time at their house while her husband was on fishing trips. During those moments, our bond deepened, and she became a cherished mentor to me.

Sadly, our time together was cut short. Circumstances changed, and she had to leave. Before saying goodbye, Missy gave me a necklace with a single pearl and said to me, "Never forget, you are a pearl." That moment became a defining memory, and the necklace became a precious keepsake I cherished deeply for years.

Her words stayed with me in a world where women often feel overlooked. That simple act of giving me the pearl necklace spoke volumes about her belief in my potential. It served as a constant reminder that I possessed a unique beauty and value, just like the pearl itself.

I share this story for a few reasons. First, it is one that came to define much of my philosophy of education. Just like the woman who saw the potential within me and nurtured it with love and wisdom, I came to see students as gems and pearls. When parents bring their children to school, they bring their best, most precious treasures and ask us to take care of them all day long and to treat them with respect, nurture them, and help them grow up. That is our job in society, to polish the pearls.

Second, it highlights something truly important about the relationship between parents, students, and learning organizations. I had loving parents who were good to me and taught me many important lessons. However, the presence, words, and attention of another adult—someone outside of my family—had a ripple effect across my life. This shows us that in order to grow into the very best versions of themselves, children need many different influences. It takes a village, as they say, and that is what this chapter is about.

The third reason is an aspect that I haven't touched on significantly in this book, yet it remains incredibly important. You see, this woman neither looked like me nor shared my upbringing. So, this moment reinforced the vital role of effective communication and collaboration across cultures, especially within the context of raising and educating children and students, caring for their holistic development, and working collectively toward a better society. As caregivers, educators, and members of the community, it is our responsibility to ensure that children are exposed to diverse perspectives and experiences. By embracing cross-cultural communication and collaboration, we provide them invaluable opportunities to develop a profound understanding and appreciation of different cultures, beliefs, and values.

Incorporating cultural diversity into our educational and caregiving practices creates an environment that nurtures the holistic growth of children. We acknowledge that each child comes from a unique cultural background, bringing with them distinct strengths, needs, and learning styles. By integrating diverse perspectives into our teaching methods, curriculum, and support systems, we can tailor our approaches to meet the individual needs of every child.

Society relies on symbiotic relationships or partnerships to grow healthy, confident children. No single entity or individual can meet all the needs of children and their families alone. We can create an inclusive and supportive environment for children to thrive through collaboration, cooperation, and active engagement with community members, organizations, and institutions. The concept of "it takes a village" underscores the interconnectedness of our efforts. It acknowledges that raising and educating children is a shared responsibility that extends beyond the immediate family. That is what we will focus on in this chapter.

DEFINE PARTNERSHIPS

Partnerships between educational institutions and various stakeholders in the community have proven to be instrumental in achieving shared goals and enhancing educational outcomes. To understand the significance of these partnerships, let's first define what partnership means in the context of education:

A partnership can be defined as a collaborative relationship between two or more entities working together toward a common purpose and shared goals. In the realm of education, partnerships involve the active engagement and cooperation between schools, educators, students, families, community organizations, businesses, and other stakeholders. These collaborations aim to leverage collective strengths, resources, and expertise to provide comprehensive support, create enriching learning experiences, and ensure the holistic development of students.

Now, let's explore several examples of successful partnerships that illustrate the power of collaboration in education:

1. Partnership between Schools and Local Businesses:

- Schools collaborate with local businesses to provide students with real-world learning experiences and career exploration opportunities.
- Businesses offer internships, mentorship programs, and guest speakers, enriching the curriculum and exposing students to different career paths.
- This partnership enhances students' understanding of the relevance of their education and fosters the development of essential workplace skills.

2. Partnership between School Districts and Community Organizations:

- School districts form partnerships with community organizations, such as non-profits and youth centers, to provide comprehensive support to students and families.
- These partnerships offer after-school programs, tutoring services, mental health resources, and access to extracurricular activities, ensuring holistic development and addressing students' diverse needs.

- By leveraging community expertise and resources, schools can create a supportive ecosystem that enhances student well-being and academic success.

3. Partnership within Professional Learning Communities:

- Educators within a school or district form PLCs to collaborate and improve instructional practices.
- PLCs provide a platform for teachers to share best practices, exchange ideas, and engage in continuous professional development.
- By working together, educators enhance their instructional strategies, align curriculum standards, and promote student-centered learning, ultimately improving student outcomes.

4. Partnership between Schools and Parents/Families:

- Schools establish partnerships with parents and families to create a strong home-to-school connection and support students' educational journey.
- Regular communication between teachers and families helps build trust, share insights about students' strengths and challenges, and foster a supportive learning environment.
- Parent involvement in school activities, volunteering opportunities, and parent-teacher associations enriches the educational experience and ensures the community being served retains its voice and presence.

These examples highlight the value of collaborative efforts, as they enrich the educational experience, broaden students' horizons, and strengthen the support system surrounding them.

Successful partnerships foster a sense of shared responsibility and collective investment in the success of every student. By engaging stakeholders from the community, schools can tap into a wealth of resources, expertise, and perspectives that enhance the educational journey and contribute to a thriving learning environment.

As an educational leader, you hold a significant role in forging, fostering, and protecting vital partnerships in education. The success of these partnerships relies on your ability to navigate the collaborative landscape and ensure their longevity and impact. To fulfill this role, consider the following key aspects of your leadership:

Setting a clear vision and direction that emphasizes the value of partnerships is crucial. By articulating the importance of collaboration and embedding it in your school's mission and strategic plans, you establish a solid foundation for meaningful partnerships to thrive. Inspire your team and stakeholders with a compelling vision that highlights the power of collective action.

Building strong relationships is another essential aspect of your leadership. Actively engage with various stakeholders, including community organizations, businesses, parents, and educators. Seek opportunities for collaboration, create channels for open communication, and establish a sense of trust and mutual respect among partners. Your ability to connect and bring people together is instrumental in fostering collaboration and collective effort.

As a facilitator and coordinator, you have the responsibility of bringing different stakeholders together and coordinating their efforts toward a common purpose. Create platforms, such as meetings, workshops, or task forces, that provide opportunities for collaboration, idea exchange, and the establishment of shared goals and action plans. Guide and support these collaborative processes, ensuring they stay focused and aligned with the overall vision of the partnership.

Resource allocation is a critical aspect of your leadership role. Advocate for the necessary resources, both financial and human, to support partnership initiatives. Recognize the importance of equitable distribution among partners, demonstrating your commitment to the partnership's success. By providing the necessary support, you create an environment where all stakeholders can contribute their unique strengths and resources.

As an advocate, you play a vital role in promoting partnerships within your educational institution and the broader community. Champion the value of collaboration, highlighting the benefits of partnerships to stakeholders, and creating policies that support partnership initiatives. Your active advocacy inspires others to embrace the collective impact that can be achieved through collaboration.

Conflict resolution is an inevitable part of partnership development. Foster open dialogue, practice active listening, and serve as a mediator when conflicts arise. Ensure that all partners feel heard, valued, and supported throughout the partnership journey. By effectively addressing conflicts, you contribute to the strength and sustainability of the partnerships you cultivate.

Evaluation and continuous improvement are essential to successful partnerships. Establish mechanisms for monitoring and evaluating the effectiveness of partnerships. Seek feedback from stakeholders, assess the impact of collaborative efforts on student outcomes, and make necessary adjustments to improve the quality and sustainability of partnerships. Constantly evaluating and refining partnership initiatives ensures their relevance and alignment with the evolving needs of your educational community.

EXAMPLES OF SUCCESSFUL PARTNERSHIPS IN EDUCATION

Partnerships in education have the potential to create transformative experiences for students, shaping their learning, well-being, and overall school success. Let's revisit the story of Little Mountain Elementary School, where a multitude of partnerships played a pivotal role in its success. This story highlights the power of partnerships in creating positive change, from the school's collaboration with Microsoft to empower education through technology to the school staff and parents' collaborative efforts to build a thriving learning community.

One notable partnership was the collaboration between the school and Microsoft. Recognizing the significance of technology in modern education, the school leader formed a strategic alliance with Microsoft, enabling students to access cutting-edge technology resources. This partnership provided students with support through the selection of state-of-the-art devices, educational software, and digital learning platforms, enhancing their engagement, critical thinking skills, and preparedness for the digital age.

This brings me to another important point about partnerships. The first is that there must be mutual benefit, especially when it comes to businesses. Microsoft was doing research into the effectiveness of its technology in a learning environment. We were looking to integrate technology into how we taught English and literacy to ELL students. There was already some alignment. The second point is that the partnership *is* an agreement, and where there is funding involved, there will be stipulations. In order to secure this partnership, we had to commit to growing our educators' skills in literacy and technology *first*. We also had to have a secondary partnership with Western Washington University and Washington State University to head up the research element under the leadership of researchers and educators like Dr. Richard Sagor and Dr. Oddmund Myhre.

Another vital partnership emerged between the district and the school staff, exemplifying the importance of shared decision-making and resource allocation. The school staff actively participated in decision-making processes through a site-based management approach, including budget allocation and resource acquisition. This collaborative effort empowered educators to identify and address the specific needs of their students, creating an optimal learning environment by effectively utilizing available resources.

The partnership between the school staff and parents was equally instrumental in shaping the success of Little Mountain Elementary School. During the school's construction phase, parents and staff members joined forces to build children's playground equipment and address various challenges. This partnership fostered a strong sense of ownership and pride within the school community, as parents witnessed their collective efforts manifest into a vibrant learning space. The involvement of parents in the construction process symbolized a deeper level of engagement and commitment to their children's education.

These examples from Little Mountain Elementary School demonstrate the diverse nature of partnerships and their profound impact on student success. The school did not become an outlier because of one person's or even one group's efforts. I've talked a lot about collaborative action so far in this book, this is the same concept at a larger scale. A partnership is about bringing together the gifts and expertise from various groups to achieve a common goal. The H.E.A.R.T I and II projects were collaborations with district leaders, staff, community, parents, university partners, and outside business partners like Lightspan, Inc. Without these partnerships being facilitated and maintained, as well as data continuously shared to show our growth, we would not have sustained the forward momentum to reach staff reading goals for students, nor would we have met the needs of our diverse community in literacy [Clauson and Myhre, 2000].

If any of these partnerships at Little Mountain Elementary School had encountered challenges, such as poor synergy or a gross imbalance of power, the consequences could have been significant and far-reaching. Consider the potential scenarios that could have unfolded if these partnerships had failed.

In the case of the collaboration between the school and Microsoft, a lack of synergy or effective communication could have hindered the successful integration of technology into the learning environment. Students might have been left without the necessary devices, software, and digital resources to support their learning. This could have limited their access to valuable educational opportunities, hindered their technological literacy, and impeded their preparedness for an increasingly digital world.

Similarly, if the partnership between the district and the school staff had faced challenges, such as an imbalance of power or ineffective resource allocation, the school's ability to meet the unique needs of its students could have been compromised. The educators might have been constrained by limited resources or unable to make decisions that best aligned with the students' interests and goals. This could have resulted in a diminished learning experience, reduced student engagement, and missed opportunities for growth and development.

Additionally, if the partnership between the school staff and parents had faltered, the sense of community and ownership within the school could have been jeopardized. Parents might have felt disconnected or disengaged from the educational process, leading to a decline in their involvement and support. This could have limited the collaborative efforts to address challenges, build a nurturing learning environment, and provide holistic support to students. The absence of strong parental involvement could have resulted in a diminished sense of belonging and hindered the school's overall success.

It is crucial to acknowledge that these partnerships' failure would have cascading effects on students' academic achievements, well-being, and overall school culture. The potential consequences could have included limited access to resources and opportunities, decreased student motivation and engagement, weakened relationships between stakeholders, and a diminished sense of belonging and support within the school community.

To mitigate these risks and ensure the success of partnerships, educational leaders play a critical role in fostering an environment of collaboration, open communication, and shared decision-making. They must actively address power imbalances, promote equitable practices, and encourage the meaningful participation of all stakeholders. By cultivating trust, fostering effective communication channels, and valuing the contributions of each partner, leaders can prevent the breakdown of partnerships and create an inclusive and empowering educational ecosystem. This brings us to our next point: what makes partnerships successful?

KEY FACTORS OF SUCCESSFUL PARTNERSHIPS

As with any relationship, successful educational partnerships are built on several key factors that create collective efforts and are aligned toward achieving shared goals. Think back to our discussion on transformational leadership. One of your jobs as a leader is to get team buy-in on one shared vision and expand ownership so team members can work together. Think about what makes that dynamic effective. The factors you need for successful collaboration within your organization are the same factors you'll have for leading a partnership between organizations. Here are the most important ones from my experience:

1. **Shared Vision and Goals:** Partnerships thrive when all stakeholders have a shared vision and a common understanding of the desired outcomes. This involves collectively defining the partnership's purpose, values, and objectives. (Remember, everyone comes to the table

and therefore has skin in the game.) By aligning their visions and goals, partners can work with a sense of purpose and direction toward meaningful and impactful student outcomes.

2. **Clear Communication:** This may seem obvious, but you'd be surprised how easily communication can break down in education. Effective communication involves open and transparent dialogue among partners, allowing for the exchange of ideas, perspectives, and information. Regular communication channels, such as meetings, emails, and shared platforms, facilitate ongoing engagement and strengthen the partnership.

3. **Trust and Mutual Respect:** This is probably the most important and under-appreciated factor on this list. Trust forms the cornerstone of successful partnerships. Building trust requires open and honest interactions, reliability, and consistency in actions and commitments. When partners trust each other, they can work collaboratively, share ideas and resources, and navigate challenges with confidence. But you cannot have trust without mutual respect. This is a recognition of the unique contributions, perspectives, and expertise of each partner. It also recognizes the importance of diversity and respect for the different cultures represented in a community or partnership. It is not doing things in isolation without gathering voices from all stakeholders involved.

4. **Complementary Strengths and Resources:** Along with mutual respect, successful partnerships leverage the diverse strengths and resources of each partner. Everyone brings unique expertise, experiences, and resources to the table. By combining their respective resources and expertise, partners can create innovative

solutions, maximize their collective impact, and provide students with enriched learning experiences.

These key factors of successful partnerships form a powerful framework for collaboration not only in education but any field. By prioritizing these factors, educational leaders can create an ecosystem that nurtures and sustains partnerships, leading to improved student outcomes, enhanced family engagement, and a stronger and more vibrant community.

RESILIENT PARTNERSHIPS

I'd like to say that collaborating in real communities was as simple as adhering to the factors I just mentioned. Unfortunately, that isn't always the case. Sometimes, that mutual respect is missing. Sometimes there are obstacles placed in the way by other stakeholders that you must overcome. Sometimes being resilient means finding new ways to reach outcomes when there is clear obstructionism. I've faced some of that in small and large districts across the country, and I've learned to be stealthy and stand firm in my values. One of the toughest realities a leader may deal with is that you won't always "fit" a community. Even if you've been brought in exactly for that reason, so you can stir up change, sometimes, community interactions are laced with judgment and prejudice that hinder effective communications or limit the ability of *everyone* to have a voice at the table. In this section, I'd like to present resilience in two ways: personal and organizational.

As leaders, we know we must be resilient to weather the storms and challenges thrown at us. But what if those challenges are driven by factors outside of our control. Most people would not know it by looking at me, but my father has Native American family, and I've spent a lot of time around tribal peoples. This has helped me be able to work with people from different backgrounds and cultures, people who didn't look or talk like me, but whom I had learned to respect. It is also a part of why I was able to work well in international schools.

Despite this, there have been occasions where my skin color has impacted how others view me. I remember a time when I was working with an up-and-coming district administrator. He was a very talented African American man who had worked very hard to get to his position. Our paths crossed through my work and I became a mentor to him. As he began new projects, he enlisted my help because he knew what I was capable of. There were other candidates for the project, some of whom were well-credentialed People of Color who weren't happy about his decision. They thought this choice was an instance of discrimination because he chose *me*, a white woman, instead of them.

I've also worked in districts where my status as a woman created obstacles for me. While I was a leader, on paper, the culture of the districts I was serving in would have preferred a white man because that is what they had been used to. They would say things like, "Here comes that woman" or "What is that little woman up to now?" In order to serve my roles best for the time, I had to learn resilience—for me, this meant compartmentalizing so I could stay the course. This meant doubling down on the tenets of transformational leadership to remain goal-oriented and produce results. (Recall our slingshot analogy from a previous chapter.) Still, I wondered if the Black woman from my childhood could see across color to recognize that I was valuable, why couldn't we do more of that for others?

While you may face obstructionists and those who would undermine you as a leader, I want to throw out the idea that no matter how targeted the attacks or obstructions may seem, they are not truly personal. People with antithetical values will make you into a symbol of what they must oppose, and you'll find they have no desire to understand you. That fact is evidence that perhaps resistance has less to do with your ability to lead than with those people's desire to remain set in their ways with as little disruption as possible. You're just in the way of that.

But, like I said, resilience is not just about personal perseverance. You want to create resilience in your organization and in your partnerships. This requires more than strength of character, but conscious effort and willingness to have the best team members regardless of where they come from. You must be willing to look for the best in other people and acknowledge that differences make us stronger.

Part of our success at Little Mountain Elementary School was our collaboration. We needed strong partnerships between the staff, the district, the local university, the tech companies, and the community as a whole. But saying "the community" is too broad a generalization because 60% of our community was non-native English speakers (ELL). The question became how do you establish a trusting and respectful relationship with people who don't even speak the same language?

Amid all the moving parts and the different entities that played a vital role in making the school a success, it became clear to me that if any of these collaborations were hindered by something as seemingly trivial as color, voice, or background, we had to find a way to overcome it. There was no one-size-fits-all approach, but it was a topic that needed to be addressed.

Thanks to the decisions made around our site-based budget, we had a team of translators and interpreters provided by the district. As the need for translation grew, we had parents who could serve as key staff members and help with translation. Whenever I met my parents, I would greet them in their language. They would respond in Spanish, and I would quickly realize that I couldn't go any further without an interpreter. It was important for me to respect their language and not make a mess of it. So, I would turn to my interpreter and translator and ask them to take over and be my voice in the parents' language. The parents noticed what I did – I welcomed them in their own language. However, I understood that I couldn't fully communicate the specifics about their child that way. The goal was to make them feel welcome, gain their trust, and allow them to share in their own language while the interpreter conveyed the message and information to both parties. This process was repeated in every public meeting.

The most powerful part came when leaders from the community started getting involved. It's something we never even talked about before. During the state tests, I would invite a parent whose child had excelled on the test, someone who was a shining example, a few years older, to come and speak to other parents in Spanish. They would share what they had done to help their child succeed. This created a platform for parents to coach each other on raising their children in America. And it worked. All we did was empower their own leaders.

In the end, it was about creating an environment of inclusivity, where language barriers were overcome, and parents were given the tools to support their children's education. Together, through partnership and collaboration, we can empower parents and students to thrive.

This sort of collaboration creates resilience in organizations, specifically in our education system, because it promotes community voice and creates an environment where everyone gets what they need to thrive. No one is sitting on a pedestal dictating what everyone else should get or do, deciding who should speak for whom and when. Instead, we allowed everyone to be their authentic selves, which fostered the trust and mutual respect needed to create stability. Our community families knew that we truly saw and valued them, and they in turn taught their children how to treat us at the school. They also took over some of the burden of preparing students and parents from their culture so that we could all grow together. And remember, that is a cornerstone of the continuous improvement cycle we discussed before.

FINAL THOUGHTS

If there were just two things you took away from this chapter regarding partnerships they should be the key factors of successful partnerships and this: we only work as well as we work together. It is said, "if you want to go fast, go alone; if you want to go far, go together." I would like to suggest that sometimes the fastest path to results is to rely on each other. Imagine it this way, how much longer would it take for you to learn the skills needed to build software than it would to hire a software engineer with a coding team? And if the goal is a software that serves an organizational need, is it more important that the person designing it speaks perfect English, or that they can give you the best results in the shortest time frame?

If we are ever going to transform our school organizations or our society into one where everyone can thrive and give their best, we must see each other's value. Diamonds, pearls, and gold are all valuable. When you put them together, they become priceless jewelry.

RESILIENCE INSIGHTS

- Resilient organizations and partnerships are built on conscious efforts to embrace diversity and acknowledge differences. Creating environments of inclusivity, where authentic voices are valued, fosters trust and mutual respect, thus contributing to the stability and overall resilience of the community or organization.

- Collaborative partnerships enhance resilience by empowering individuals within the community. By involving parents, local leaders, and diverse stakeholders, organizations create an environment where everyone's needs are met, trust is built, and mutual growth is facilitated, reflecting the essence of the continuous improvement cycle.
- Effective leaders remain steadfast in their values, finding innovative ways to overcome hindrances and maintain focus on the mission and vision for their community.
- Resilient partnerships emphasize the importance of working together for collective success. Leadership is not about going fast alone but progressing far together. Valuing each other's strengths and diverse perspectives is essential for transformation.

8

COMMUNITY VOICE

"One light feeds another. One strong family lends strength to more. One engaged community can ignite those around it. This is the power of the light we carry."

— *MICHELLE OBAMA*

In the previous chapter, we explored the importance of effective communication and inclusivity in engaging with diverse communities as it relates to successful partnerships. I shared an example of how using interpreters and translators at Little Mountain Elementary School, in conjunction with greeting families in their native tongue, enabled us to bridge the language barrier and engage with Spanish-speaking families. This approach demonstrated mutual respect, acknowledging the value of different cultures and the importance of empowering individuals to express their own perspectives. We applied the same approach to opening an American International School in Doha, Qatar, and after eight years, the school is sustained and serving its children.

These examples exemplified the concept of community voice—the driving force behind this chapter's discussion.

Throughout this book, we've been setting the stage to talk about community voice. In Chapter 3, we dove into the qualities of influential leaders who empower others and embrace diverse perspectives, laying the foundation for understanding the power of community voice in amplifying collective wisdom and collaboration. Then, Chapters 4 and 5 touched on the importance of collaborative action and creative tension, which rely on effective communication and collective ownership of outcomes. And Chapter 6, we shed some light on the challenges and opportunities presented by diverse communities, emphasizing the importance of cultural responsiveness and valuing each individual's unique experiences. In this chapter, we'll explore the intersectionality of community voice with other concepts such as social justice, equity, and inclusivity as essential elements to understanding the broader impact and significance of community voice within a societal context (as well as why this is important to us).

WHAT IS "COMMUNITY VOICE"?

Community voice can be considered the collective expression of individuals within a community. It goes beyond tokenism and seeks to empower individuals to actively participate in decision-making processes, program development, and policy formulation. By embracing community voice, we recognize that all threads of our societal tapestry hold equal value, regardless of their color or background. The concept of community voice extends beyond mere inclusion; it acknowledges every individual's inherent worth and unique contributions within a community. Creating spaces where people can freely express their ideas and experiences opens doors to new perspectives, innovative solutions, and collaborative opportunities.

As an education leader, understanding the importance of community voice is vital. It's the foundation of collaboration, partnership, and transformational leadership. Actively seeking input from students, parents, teachers, and the community provides insights into their needs and aspirations. This helps shape policies and practices aligned with community values, fostering buy-in, ownership, and shared responsibility for outcomes. It signifies a collaborative effort.

More importantly, community voice allows one to address disparities and inequities within the education system. It allows us to identify and dismantle systemic barriers that may hinder certain voices from being heard or represented. By actively engaging with historically marginalized communities and individuals, we can work toward creating a more inclusive and equitable learning environment. We saw this at Little Mountain and in places like Doha, Qatar; Oakland, CA; and, more recently, Seattle, WA. To make this more grounded, here's a thought experiment:

Let's say an analysis of your school district reveals above-average rates of obesity, terminated pregnancy, and mental health emergencies among teens ages 12 to 15. (I know these may sound drastic, but hopefully, you can see how these issues are important, relevant, and contentious.) In response, there is a proposal to update the health curriculum. The aim is to provide a comprehensive education that addresses these pressing issues and promotes the well-being of students. Take a moment and think about this. What would be the best approach to decide on the new course material and roll out the curriculum for the coming school year?

If you thought it through, you might have found it more challenging the more you turned it over. There is not a single, simple answer on which to fall back. Let me give you two scenarios of how this process *could* go:

When Community Voice is Not Acknowledged:
District administration decides to implement the new curriculum without seeking input from teachers, students, and parents. The decision is made behind closed doors, without transparency or engagement with the community. The curriculum is rolled out without considering the diverse needs, preferences, and concerns of those directly impacted by it. As a result, teachers feel disempowered and frustrated, students struggle to connect with the material, and parents feel excluded from the decision-making process. The lack of acknowledgement of community voice creates a sense of mistrust, resistance, and a disconnection between the administration and the community.

When Community Voice is Acknowledged:
The district takes a collaborative approach by establishing a Health Education Task Force, comprising teachers, parents, students, healthcare professionals, and community members. Through town hall meetings and online surveys, the district actively seeks input and feedback from stakeholders, incorporating their perspectives into the curriculum design. Transparent communication is maintained, keeping the community informed about the progress and how their input has shaped the final curriculum. The result is a sense of shared ownership, where teachers, students, and parents feel valued and empowered. Students receive a relevant and rigorous education that addresses their unique needs, leading to increased engagement and improved health outcomes. This collaborative process fosters a stronger sense of well-being within the school community.

In these examples, the difference lies in the level of involvement, transparency, and respect. To be fair, given the nature of the subject matter, it is unlikely that any attempts to address these specific problems would be met without a fair amount of backlash.

There will be many opinions on how they should be handled, and whose responsibility it is. Some will be culturally based while others may be data-driven. The point is that in a transformational leadership model the decision of "what's best for students" is not made unilaterally and dictated from the top down. It recognizes the problem exists *and* it invites other perspectives on how best to address them.

For issues that generate a lot of passionate uproar, it's important to remain resilient and remember that it's not just about what we believe. As leaders, we aren't here to fix or prescribe, but remove obstacles. You may be tempted to make the decision in a top-down fashion, alienating parents and teachers by forcing a curriculum that matches the direction you think schools should go. You risk trying to stretch your community too far too fast. But if you involve the community, you learn how far you can stretch your slingshot and open up the possibility for creative tension to occur, fostering creative new ideas.

COMMUNITY VOICE AND MARGINALIZATION

In community settings, the dynamics between the dominant culture and minoritized cultures can significantly impact the distribution of power and decision-making. When the dominant culture holds overwhelming decision-making power, it can lead to marginalization and perpetuate systemic inequalities. Community voice initiatives play a crucial role in combating this and promoting inclusivity and equity.

One of the key problems that arise when the dominant culture monopolizes decision-making is the silencing of minoritized voices. Before I go any further, I feel it is vital to clarify what I mean by "minoritized" in the context of societal structure, influence, and opportunity. It is common to use the word "minority" when referring to many nonwhite communities and social groups.

The problem with that term is that it implies that those people are "less than" either in value or in number. In reality, no one is lesser in value, and often the numbers (regarding population) are not "less." In many places across the United States, White people are in "the minority." So you can see the term is problematic at best.

What we are actually referring to are social groups that have been historically marginalized. This is in recognition of the systemic power imbalances that have persisted throughout US history and even today, leading to the underrepresentation and disenfranchisement of various communities, specifically Black, Latinx, Indigenous, Asian, and immigrant families. This concept acknowledges that these racial, ethnic, and social groups have and continue to face structural/systemic injustices, discrimination, and unequal access to resources and opportunities.

I want to reframe it in your mind as **structural minoritization,** acknowledging the persistent biases, practices, and structures within a community that systematically disadvantage certain groups, regardless of the demographic makeup of that community. It takes into account how biases and favoritism are perpetuated through established systems, institutions, and social norms that are too often the present-day status quo.

I have lived and worked in places where the educational leadership did not (at least initially) reflect the demographic makeup due to historical disparities in education and access. Historically marginalized communities were often underrepresented and underserved in these places because their voices were not respected. I have also lived and worked in communities where historically marginalized groups (such as African American and Latinx) were the demographic majority and held insignificant influence over decisions in their communities due to underrepresentation.

This may seem like splitting hairs, but here's why it matters: when working to promote community voice, you must know the makeup of your district. Who are your students and families? Who are your decision-makers? Who is excluded or neglected? What is the status quo? What are the barriers to opportunity (and how can you disrupt them)? You must acknowledge the historical marginalization and minoritization of certain groups in this country that persist today and how those dynamics impact your community. If you don't pay attention to your community makeup, you risk perpetuating practices that allow students furthest from success and opportunity to remain excluded.

This exclusion prevents the development of a truly inclusive and representative decision-making process that acknowledges and supports all students and families. The "minoritized" groups are not only left out of dialogue that impacts them but also become vulnerable to hate speech and deliberate undermining of their needs. They become viewed as the problem rather than having their experiences validated and responded to through targeted, meaningful intervention. Here is another thought experiment:

Imagine attending a town hall meeting or open forum meeting for the proposed curriculum change from my previous example. Imagine English is neither your first nor strongest language. What might it be like trying to participate if all of the leaders and presenters speak only English? Imagine yourself and other concerned parents asking for more interpreters or a translation, only to be told that you should learn better English... How valued and respected, would you feel in that environment? How much trust would you have that your child's best interest is being considered?

If community leadership doesn't even account for the different languages spoken by stakeholders, how understanding do you think they are in addressing the unique challenges faced by ELL students in predominantly white, English-Speaking schools? What else is allowed to slip through the cracks?

When the community as a whole does not have a voice in the decisions that affect them, the people who are most vulnerable get stuck on the fringes and fall through the cracks. And when it comes time to address a concern that impacts them, initiatives get created like directives being forced upon them rather than collaboratively developed opportunities to uplift them based on their needs. We cannot presume to know what others are going through without walking a mile in their shoes or at least listening to *their* journey. As a leader who will serve many different people, part of your role will be to create opportunities for *all* stakeholders to voice their experiences, concerns, and needs.

This reminds me of a time when I worked at an elementary school during a head-lice breakout. It was so bad the lice were spreading to students from their coats and bags. In an attempt to protect all students (and staff), the Health Department issued a strategy involving regular head-lice checks and education for parents. This was a government-regulated directive that had to be implemented to protect everyone, and we were all concerned.

During these check-ups, students were removed from class. The ones who were "clean" returned, while those who weren't got sent home. The school where I worked was a uniquely diverse school community with students, including a significant population of Latinx and English Bilingual students and families. Since all parents were concerned for student health and on board with the Health Department's intervention plan, we wanted to ensure our school implemented the policy in a respectful and inclusive way for everyone and did not give the image of some groups being clean or unclean. It was important to us at this school that we tackled these tough issues across race and language together. (This was how we approached tests and other things like test preparation too.)

Because the protocol required educating parents and families about hygiene and how to clean their homes, we felt it was important to empower all communities to implement this training while honoring prevalent languages and relationships. Perhaps you can imagine how invasive and insulting this would look if it were implemented without the inclusion of all communities. Instead of dictating a solution to them, we needed to empower everyone to be leaders in this. So we invited parents, mentors, and leaders from the community and provided everyone with the necessary knowledge and skills to teach and lead change in a dignified manner.

As I said, it was in our site culture to tackle tough problems together. Unfortunately, this is not always the case. Sometimes, when administrators, political leaders, and activists try to create change *without* actually involving the impacted families from the start, it starts to look like "white saviorism." This was not an "us helping them" scenario. It rarely is, and you must avoid that type of thinking when engaging diverse and marginalized communities.

Embracing community voice and shared leadership had a transformative impact on the school and the community as a whole. It allowed for more collaborative problem-solving and supported ongoing engagement from all stakeholders. It focused on relationships and didn't make any group feel isolated or dictated to. Staff members and community leaders were instrumental in driving change and contributing to the success of the school from the start. Through their efforts, we achieved remarkable progress in various areas, empowering individuals to take ownership of their experiences and voices.

MODERATING COMMUNITY VOICE

As a leader, you will be crucial in moderating voices and ensuring that all perspectives are heard. Sometimes certain voices can get very loud, disruptive, and even disrespectful. Too often, the loudest, most persistent voices get what they want at the expense of everyone else. What should you do when some voices may be potentially harmful or overshadow others? How do you all voices have representation while mitigating the potential for damage?

Here are some strategies that leaders can try. They are not the only ones, nor are they mutually exclusive. The point is not to prescribe one best practice but provide some ideas to help you:

- **Set Clear Guidelines:** Begin discussions by establishing clear guidelines for respectful communication and diverse participation. These guidelines create a safe space where everyone's voice matters, fostering constructive dialogue from the start.
- **Facilitate Actively:** Lead conversations with active facilitation to ensure equal participation. Encourage quieter voices, manage the flow of discussion, and promote diverse viewpoints. By balancing the conversation, you create an environment where every perspective shines.
- **Structure Engagement:** Shape engagement by incorporating small group discussions and diverse interaction formats. Breakout sessions and rotating facilitation roles allow for inclusive conversations, ensuring that various voices are heard.
- **Practice Listening and Empathy:** Model active listening and empathy to foster an atmosphere of understanding. Show genuine interest in different viewpoints, inviting others to do the same. Paraphrasing, asking clarifying questions, and summarizing ideas demonstrate your commitment to respectful dialogue.
- **Challenge Harmful Narratives:** Be vigilant in addressing harmful narratives or hate speech promptly. Uphold a zero-tolerance approach to discriminatory

behavior. Redirect conversations if they become disrespectful, keeping the focus on constructive and inclusive dialogue.

- **Balance Collaboration and Protection:** Strike a balance between encouraging collaboration and protecting against harmful content. Proactively address harmful speech, enforcing guidelines that ensure everyone's safety and well-being.
- **Create Safe Spaces:** Establish platforms for confidential or anonymous contributions to encourage open dialogue without fear of judgment. Providing channels for feedback and anonymous input empowers diverse perspectives to be shared openly.
- **Uphold Values:** Stay committed to your organization's values, even when facing opposition. Ensure decisions align with inclusivity, equity, and respect. Don't compromise the well-being of your community by giving in to dominant voices. Trust your decisions when they serve the greater good.

As leaders, we are responsible for navigating the complexities of moderating voices and managing potentially harmful narratives within our communities. While ensuring that all voices are heard is crucial, it is important to recognize that not every opinion, even if it represents the majority, is necessarily the right one. There is a difference between those trying to be heard and those trying to drown out everyone else. Our role is to create an environment and culture where individuals feel respected and valued, allowing for a range of opinions to be expressed without fear. We may encounter resistance from louder or more established voices, but we must remain steadfast in our decision to serve *all* and empower those who have historically fallen through the cracks. This isn't speaking for them, but giving them the stage and passing the feather.

COMMUNITY VOICE PAVES THE WAY FOR CHANGE

The last thing I want to do in this chapter is share with you *one more* reason it is important to consider community voice: it paves the way for change. In a society, when a dominant group or culture holds too much power, they are able to dictate the narrative and decide on what resources and opportunities each social group gets access to. Nothing can change as long as the same voice remains louder than the others. This is a part of the beauty of the true servanthood of Dr. Martin Luther King's leadership model.

Dr. King's work is an example of community voice in action, challenging power dynamics and systemic inequality. During the Civil Rights Movement, Dr. King emerged as one of many courageous leaders advocating for racial justice and equality. At that time, society was deeply entrenched in power imbalances and systemic racism. Black, brown, Indigenous, and immigrant communities faced discrimination, segregation, and limited opportunities.

Dr. King's leadership sought to dismantle these power dynamics by empowering marginalized communities to raise their voices against injustice. His approach emphasized the power of collective action and grassroots organizing. He understood that marginalized voices needed to be amplified and that true change could only occur when the community had a seat at the table. Dr. King's work involved engaging community members, encouraging them to share their stories, and fostering solidarity among diverse groups affected by systemic inequality. And it was not just African Americans. For instance, many of the garbage workers he engaged with were white and poor. By bringing them in and adding their voices to the shared movement, they became greater and their efforts more effective.

By amplifying community voices, Dr. King challenged the dominance of the status quo and pushed for policies and practices that promoted equality and justice. His leadership and activism paved the way for significant advancements in civil rights and inspired generations of activists to continue the fight against discrimination and oppression.

Last, I want to add that I use Dr. King's example because he was a powerful, intentional leader who modeled ideals that I respect and aspire to. It is easy to speak highly about his actions. While we look to his example, let us not forget that he was met with a lot of resistance. He became a martyr. His dream, of which he spoke so passionately, is still being worked and fought for. That is why we are talking about this now. Today, there are still implications and barriers for marginalized communities to overcome in large part because their voices have not been represented, included, or respected. As leaders in education, we need to prioritize engaging with and embracing the voices of our marginalized, minoritized communities if we hope to create thriving learning communities.

As you reflect on your role as a leader, I want to invite you to think about who you are serving. What are your priorities and how do they measure up to the needs of your communities? How well are your community's needs and perspectives represented in the decision-making process? And finally, what are some specific strategies or tactics you can employ to *give voice* back to your stakeholders? (I.E. how can you gather information you don't have from people who will be impacted by your leadership?)

RESILIENCE INSIGHTS

- Building more resilient schools means recognizing the learning environment beyond the walls of the school and striving to obtain input from all voices. Promoting community voice establishes greater trust, which is essential for stable partnerships between families and schools.

- As a leader, you must cultivate a strong sense of self and commitment to a higher purpose. As you strive to involve more voices in important discussions, you will face resistance from multiple directions; understand that your response cannot be reactive. It would be best if you stayed centered and model the dialogue you wish to create – while having the courage to guard against harmful speech.

9
GROUP GOAL SETTING

"Coming together is the beginning. Keeping together is progress. Working together is success."

— *HENRY FORD*

A s we approach the end of this guide, I want you to imagine something with me. Picture this:

An English teacher walks onto campus at the start of the day, a little bounce in her step as she strides to her classroom to prepare the day's activities. The excitement is pouring off her because the night before, she graded her students' writing assignments and noticed a fourth straight week of improvement in creative nonfiction writing. As she approaches her door, she passes her colleagues in the English department, chattering about their students and lesson plans. Their body language is relaxed, and there's a notable sense of camaraderie in the halls.

She enters her classroom and smiles at all the desks arranged in small clusters facing each other. It is a better setup for group activities. She hadn't been allowed to do it before because it was a departure from the traditional classroom setup.

"How can students focus on your lesson if they aren't facing you?" The principal had asked in a staff meeting just weeks ago. She explained that she wanted to change her fundamental teaching style from lecture-based to activity-based. Instead of standing in the front of the classroom, she would spend more time moving between groups. This would allow her to give students more personalized support as they practiced writing and critiquing. She explained it would also give her a better pulse of where each student struggled, informing future class lessons and activities.

The other teachers in the English department had agreed and asked for more freedom to manage their classrooms in a way that played to their strengths. The principal had them draw up plans with what they would try, how they would monitor and assess, and what the expected outcome would be and encouraged them to share results and interventions before reporting on findings after forty-five days.

Her idea had been considered and used to springboard a department-wide experiment. As she begins thumbing through papers to lay out for the day's activity, she can't help but feel like she is making a meaningful contribution. That is something she hadn't felt in a long time...

This scenario represents a school that has implemented many of the concepts of this book and allowed classroom teachers to share in the leadership, ownership, and implementation of initiatives to promote student growth. Put simply, the acknowledgment of their voices and empowerment to lead their own research projects with students with support from their principal created an environment where educators were not just following the leader but feel good about contributing to the overall vision and mission.

Idyllic though it may be (and I'm sure we would all like this picture-perfect scenario!), this vignette highlights the power of community voice and collaborative action. But one thing it doesn't cover is how a team-based mindset doesn't start or stop with just implementation. Shared leadership implies some level of shared decision-making. So in this chapter, we're going to explore how inviting group participation in the goal-setting process can strengthen the resolve of the team and positively impact both the culture of your organization and the outcomes you can reach.

UNDERSTANDING THE FOUNDATIONS OF GROUP GOAL-SETTING

Group goal-setting in education involves a collaborative process where educators establish common objectives and targets to guide their efforts toward desired outcomes. This approach recognizes the value of collective wisdom and collaboration in driving educational improvement, fostering a culture of teamwork and shared ownership.

Transformational leaders facilitate this process by providing visionary leadership, motivation, and guidance to empower educators to actively participate in the goal-setting process. They create the environment of trust and open communication needed for shared decision-making. If you want to lead transformation in your organization, you will want to enable effective collaboration and co-creation of meaningful goals aligned with the organization's mission and values.

Rooted in the idea of community voice within an organization, group goal-setting relies on and drives the principles of collaborative action research, emphasizing a systematic approach to address educational challenges through shared goals. By employing research-based practices, collecting and analyzing data, and implementing targeted interventions, educators engage in a continuous improvement cycle to enhance student learning outcomes.

That's a formal way of saying just like educators use data-driven decision-making to evaluate the effectiveness of strategies and interventions. They can also use this methodology to determine areas of focus. And as educators collaborate, innovate, and share findings, they can work collectively toward a shared vision of educational excellence. This leadership approach inspires teams to embrace new ideas, take risks, and challenge the status quo, providing the necessary support and resources for educators to achieve their goals and positively impact student learning outcomes.

You can think of it as having the following phases:

- **Data Analysis:** As a group, gather and analyze relevant data and information. Engage in discussions to gain a comprehensive understanding of the current situation. Encourage everyone to share their insights, observations, and interpretations of the data. This collaborative analysis helps the team develop a shared understanding of the strengths and challenges.
- **Identifying Areas for Growth:** Facilitate a group discussion to identify areas for growth based on the data analysis. Encourage active participation from all members, ensuring that everyone's perspectives are heard and valued. Through open dialogue, prioritize the areas that require attention and align them with the organization's mission and goals. Consensus-building and constructive debate can be valuable in this process.
- **Setting SMART Goals:** Collaboratively define SMART goals that are specific, measurable, achievable, relevant, and time-bound. Ensure that the goals are aligned with the identified areas for growth. Encourage the group to

discuss and clarify the objectives, making sure they are clear and well-defined. Allow for brainstorming and creative thinking to generate ideas and strategies that will contribute to the achievement of the goals.

- **Developing Action Plans:** Once the goals are established, work together to develop action plans. Break down the goals into smaller, manageable tasks and assign responsibilities to team members based on their strengths and expertise. Encourage collaboration and cooperation among the team members, fostering a sense of shared ownership. Develop a timeline and establish checkpoints to monitor progress and ensure accountability.

The key focus here is that you and your team are collectively looking at the data to determine areas for growth. This is the beginning of collaborative inquiry.

ELEMENTS OF TEAM OWNERSHIP

You may be saying, "I get that, but how do I get my team working together like this if we have never done it this way before?" When it comes to transforming a school into a collaborative and empowering learning community, there isn't a one-size-fits-all approach. However, there are strategies and tactics that school leaders can employ to encourage team ownership, amplify different voices, and foster a culture of shared leadership. This section is devoted to exploring a few of those. First, you must understand the essential components of group goal-setting:

1. **Collaborative Culture:** Creating a collaborative culture is foundational to encouraging team ownership and shared decision-making. It begins by fostering an

environment of trust and open communication, where team members feel safe to express their opinions and ideas. Active participation and input from all team members should be encouraged, ensuring that everyone's voice is heard and valued. Promoting shared responsibility and ownership in decision-making helps establish a collective mindset where the entire team is invested in the outcomes.

2. **Valuing Different Voice:** To create an inclusive decision-making process, valuing and incorporating different voices is important. This involves creating opportunities for diverse perspectives to be heard and actively seeking input from all team members, including teachers, staff, and other stakeholders. Each individual's viewpoint should be respected and considered in the decision-making process, fostering a culture that celebrates diversity and appreciates the richness that different perspectives bring.

3. **Leveraging Team Expertise:** Recognizing and leveraging the expertise of team members is essential for effective decision-making. School leaders should identify and acknowledge the unique strengths and expertise that each team member brings to the table. Providing opportunities for team members to contribute their skills and knowledge enhances the quality of decision-making and empowers individuals to take leadership roles in areas aligned with their expertise. By capitalizing on the team's collective expertise, leaders can harness the full potential of their staff and drive meaningful change. One thing you can try for this is dividing team members into problem-solving groups: This approach allows individuals to focus on specific

challenges and contribute their knowledge and skills effectively.

4. **Fostering Teamwork:** Collaboration and teamwork are crucial for successful group goal-setting and decision-making. Leaders should encourage collaboration and cooperation among team members, fostering an environment where ideas are freely shared, and collective efforts are celebrated. Team members should be encouraged to share insight, discuss their projects, seek results, and celebrate shared successes.

No matter which tactic you use, these elements must be present for group goal-setting to be successful within your organization.

KEEP THE WHEEL TURNING

The last thing I want to emphasize is the ongoing nature of group goal-setting. It is not a one-time event but rather an ongoing process that requires regular check-ins, progress monitoring, and adjustments along the way. It should be viewed as part of the continuous improvement cycle, where educators constantly reflect, learn, and refine their goals and action plans.

Regular check-ins with their PLCs provide an invaluable opportunity for educators to assess their progress, evaluate the effectiveness of strategies, and make necessary adjustments. These check-ins allow educators to collaborate with their colleagues, share insights, and learn from each other's experiences. Through open and honest discussions, educators can gain new perspectives, challenge their assumptions, and generate innovative ideas to enhance their practices.

Reflection and feedback play a vital role in the ongoing group goal-setting process. Educators self-reflect, examining their practices and their impact on student learning. They also receive input from their colleagues and stakeholders, who provide valuable feedback and different perspectives. This feedback serves as a catalyst for growth and improvement, helping educators refine their goals, adjust their strategies, and enhance their instructional practices.

Approaching adjustments and adaptations with a growth mindset is essential in the ongoing group goal-setting process. Educators should view changes as opportunities for learning and improvement rather than as setbacks or failures. They need to embrace a mindset that values flexibility, resilience, and continuous growth. By doing so, they can leverage the power of reflection, feedback, and collaboration to continually refine their goals, implement effective strategies, and achieve meaningful student outcomes.

By understanding the ongoing nature of group goal-setting, educators can foster a culture of continuous improvement within their PLCs. They create an environment where reflection, collaboration, and adaptability are valued and celebrated. These components create a regenerative environment that builds resilience within the members through transformative practice. Remember, the transformative cycle builds a stronger muscle for continuous improvement.

This is a process that builds hope and trust within the organization and its members by driving momentum. Continuous improvement and transformational leadership are about building on what you discover, celebrating wins, and seeking to address opportunities and advance positive outliers. In this model, team members can feel greater ownership in the gains the team is building, which is how we start to build environments like the one that opened this chapter.

RESILIENCE INSIGHTS

- Establishing a collaborative culture within educational organizations promotes resilience by fostering trust, open communication, and shared responsibility. When team members feel safe to express their opinions and ideas, they are more likely to work together effectively, adapt to challenges, and collectively pursue goals.

- Recognizing and valuing different voices contributes to resilient leadership. Incorporating diverse perspectives in group goal-setting encourages creative problem-solving, enriches decision-making, and helps create an inclusive environment where all stakeholders feel heard and valued.

- Resilient leadership involves recognizing and capitalizing on the expertise of team members. By acknowledging individual strengths and providing opportunities for team members to contribute their skills, leaders empower their teams to take ownership of challenges and decisions. This approach maximizes potential and promotes adaptability in the face of change.

10

THE MENTOR ARRIVES

"When the student is ready, the master appears."

— ATTRIBUTED TO BUDDHIST PROVERB

Mentorship is a timeless practice that has played a crucial role in personal and professional growth throughout history. The guidance, support, and wisdom shared between mentors and mentees have paved the way for achievements, discoveries, and transformations. In this chapter, we delve into the art of mentorship and explore its profound impact on both mentors and mentees.

Each of us has experienced the influence of mentors in our lives. They are the lights that illuminate our paths, offering insights and wisdom that shape our perspectives and aspirations. They are guides who walk alongside us to keep us moving toward goals. Whether in academia, business, sports, or any other realm, mentorship is a powerful force that empowers individuals to unlock their full potential.

However, mentorship is not solely about imparting knowledge

or providing guidance. It is an intricate dance of connection, understanding, and growth. Mentoring relationships are built on mutual trust, respect, and shared goals, creating a nurturing environment where mentees can flourish. The role of a mentor is not merely to direct and instruct but to inspire and uplift, guiding mentees to discover their own unique paths. Throughout this chapter, we will explore the nuances of mentorship to unpack questions like, "What does it mean to be a mentor?" "Why is mentorship vital?" "How do you pick a mentor?" and "How do you know you're ready for mentorship?"

DEFINING A MENTOR

A mentor is a trusted and experienced individual who provides guidance, support, and wisdom to a mentee. Drawing from their professional knowledge and personal experiences, they offer a unique perspective to help mentees navigate their personal and professional journeys. Mentors serve as role models, offering valuable advice, encouragement, and feedback to help mentees make informed decisions and overcome challenges. A mentor possesses subject matter expertise and excellent communication and interpersonal skills.

The mentor-mentee relationship is built on trust and creates a safe space for open dialogue and mutual learning. They listen actively, empathize with the mentees' experiences and empower mentees to discover their strengths, explore their potential, and build the necessary skills and confidence to succeed. This safe space is crucial because a mentor can facilitate learning in a way that doesn't expose the mentee's weak points. Imagine if every time you needed to learn something or wanted to strengthen a skill you feel self-conscious about, you had to share that shortcoming with your supervisor or colleagues. Not everyone needs to see your development process; a good mentor knows that is why they are needed.

One common question is, "What's the difference between a mentor and a coach?" Coaches and mentors actually share several key similarities in their roles. First, they both provide supportive guidance, offering assistance and encouragement to individuals as they navigate challenges and work toward their goals. Additionally, coaches and mentors prioritize relationship building, fostering a sense of trust and creating an open space for communication and collaboration. Both roles are also oriented toward goal-setting, with coaches and mentors helping individuals define and pursue specific objectives while providing accountability and motivation. Moreover, coaches and mentors are invested in personal development, promoting self-reflection and continuous learning.

While a coach and mentor are part of an individual's professional development and success circle, they perform their roles differently. Coaches primarily focus on performance improvement and goal achievement, following a structured process, while mentors prioritize overall personal and professional development, providing guidance based on their experiences. Coaching engagements are often time-bound and goal-oriented, while mentorship relationships can be long-term and enduring, extending beyond specific goals.

You can think of it like this: When you bring a challenge to a mentor, they may hold up a mirror to help you reflect on your thoughts and challenges, offering guidance and advice based on their own experiences. Coaches, on the other hand, actively work with clients to analyze problems, set goals, and develop action plans. They focus on facilitating goal achievement, taking a hands-on approach to support clients in taking concrete actions and achieving desired outcomes. While mentors provide guidance and insights, coaches prioritize action and progress.

SHOULD YOU SEEK A MENTOR?

Finding a mentor is a crucial step for every leader's continued development.   By seeking a mentor, you open yourself up to a wealth of knowledge and experiences that can accelerate your progress and success. It is an investment in yourself and your future. In some cases, mentors are readily available through established channels.

For principals and superintendents, programs and initiatives are facilitated by the state that provide access to mentors specifically tailored to the needs of educational leaders. In the State of Washington, this is facilitated through WASA (Washington Association of School Administrators) and AWSP (Association of Washington School Principals).These programs recognize the importance of mentorship in fostering effective leadership and offer avenues for mentorship connections to be made. Taking advantage of these resources can greatly enhance your ability to be effective as you progress in your career.

However, it's worth noting that you don't always have to actively seek out a mentor. As Delano Lewis discussed in his book, *It All Begins with Self*, sometimes a mentor will appear when certain signs indicate your readiness. He says:

> *"In many cases, just by being open to mentorship and showing how good and capable you are or showing your willingness to learn, a mentor will find you. People want their organizations and companies to succeed and reach their goals. If you can understand and participate in that, a mentor will find you. Then they will begin to give you coaching, advice, and guidance on how both of you can win."*

—Delano Lewis (2015).

It could be your demonstrated passion, commitment, or thirst for learning that catches the attention of a mentor, or it could be your reputation and consistent results. It could be they see themselves in you, or they see the road ahead and want to offer some protection. When they recognize your potential and see your genuine desire for development, they may reach out and offer their guidance. This organic approach to mentorship often brings about meaningful connections and transformative experiences.

When considering a mentor, it's essential to look for specific qualities and attributes that align with your goals and values. A good mentor should possess relevant experience and expertise in your field or areas of interest. They should be a good listener, empathetic, and able to provide guidance and support tailored to your needs. Trust and confidentiality are essential, as you should feel comfortable sharing your challenges, aspirations, and vulnerabilities with them. A mentor should inspire and challenge you, encouraging growth and pushing you to achieve your full potential.

In this case, your responsibility is to be open to mentorship. It is not about winning alone but developing relationships that allow you to thrive. Your success reflects on the mentor and benefits the primary stakeholders – the students.

How to Know A Mentor is Right for You

I have had many mentors, and they have always found me at the time of both greatest need and readiness. Knowing if a mentor is right for you involves considering several factors. Here are some key considerations to determine whether a mentor is a good fit:

1. Expertise and Experience: Assess if the mentor has relevant knowledge and experience in the areas you want to develop. Look for someone who has achieved what you aspire to achieve and can offer valuable insights and guidance.

2. Shared Values and Vision: Determine if the mentor's values align with yours and if their vision for success resonates with you. A mentor who shares similar values and goals can provide meaningful guidance that aligns with your aspirations.

3. Communication and Rapport: Evaluate the mentor's communication style and assess if it resonates with you. A good mentor should be able to establish rapport and effectively communicate ideas, advice, and feedback in a way that you understand and find helpful.

4. Availability and Commitment: Consider if the mentor has the time and commitment to invest in the mentorship relationship. A mentor who is available and dedicated to your growth can provide consistent guidance and support.

5. Trust and Compatibility: Trust is crucial in a mentor-mentee relationship. Assess if you feel comfortable being open and vulnerable with the mentor. Compatibility in terms of personality, values, and communication styles can also contribute to a successful mentoring experience.

6. Track Record of Success: Look at the mentor's track record of helping others succeed. If they have a history of supporting and guiding individuals toward their goals, it indicates their effectiveness as a mentor.

By carefully considering these factors, you can determine if a mentor is the right fit for you and if they can provide the guidance and support you need. And that is the important part. It is not all about reputation and accomplishment. It's about alignment, both in values and direction. In my career, I have been approached by mentors who saw my potential and wanted to work with me, but they didn't necessarily align with my values, so I declined. I've also known successful leaders approached for mentorship by other leaders who shared their values but didn't have the experience they needed for their direction.

I say all of that to remind you that it is okay not to walk through every door that presents itself to you. It is good to have a mentor, but it is better to have the right mentor. Let your actions, attitudes, and values attract the right mentors to you.

BECOMING A MENTOR

Becoming a mentor is a natural progression for transformational leaders committed to their team members' growth and development. As a transformational leader, you are already engaged in mentoring and guiding others within your team. You actively support and invest in the success of your team members, providing them with guidance, feedback, and opportunities for growth. Mentorship within your team doesn't have to be formal; it happens organically as you embody the role of a mentor on a regular basis.

Building trust and establishing a strong connection with your team members is essential. You create a safe and supportive environment where open communication flourishes. Your team members feel comfortable sharing their challenges, aspirations, and vulnerabilities, knowing that you are there to guide and support them. You demonstrate empathy, actively listen, and provide constructive feedback, fostering a sense of trust and connection. This form of leadership *is* mentorship.

As a transformational leader, you understand the importance of continuous learning and development. You actively invest in the growth of your team members, providing them with opportunities to learn, encouraging their development, and empowering them to reach their full potential. If you're not sure whether you're effective or not, here is something to keep in mind: when you're ready to be a mentor, people will start asking you questions. This indicates that others recognize your expertise and value your insights, seeking your guidance and advice. When people seek you out for your knowledge and experience, and when you find yourself naturally providing guidance and support to others, it is a sign that you are ready to embrace the role of a mentor. The interest and trust expressed by others reflect their belief in your ability to guide and mentor them effectively.

MENTORSHIP CREATES RESILIENCE

In the mentorship chapter of his book, Delano Lewis implies that mentorship strengthens the organization as a whole. The team wins because you are a successful contributor to the organization's goals. In my experience, this is completely true. We are only as great as our lowest common denominator, and by investing in ourselves and our teams, we strengthen our ranks.

As a transformational leader, that is a part of your mission—to create depth and strength within your organization. You want to set them up for success, to carry on even if you can't lead. You aren't growing followers but building more leaders who can drive the continuous improvement cycle. As you develop your team's culture of collaboration, you empower them to be curious, investigate opportunities, develop solutions, and grow each other. In other words, your team of leaders become mentors to each other, new team members, and even students. And that is why a transformational leader is needed.

As you receive mentorship, you engage in a safe space to reflect and seek advice and even coverage. Sometimes a mentor can see when you are pushing too hard or coming against obstacles that are too big to tackle alone. They will recognize the signs of burnout and help you avoid it. They can also help you bypass challenges that might leave you stressed and lost. You can think of a mentor as an anchor to keep you from drifting. Additionally, mentors provide encouragement, motivation, and emotional support, bolstering your confidence and belief in your abilities. This is a form of refueling that is essential to your longevity.

FINAL THOUGHT

I want to close this chapter with one thought: mentorship is an honor, not a burden. To be seen as valuable, needed, and useful— to have one's achievements and life experience recognized is rewarding. A mentor's greatest aspiration is to see their mentees succeed and be able to pay it forward. I will never forget the words of one of my most influential mentors, Dr. Shirley Holloway, as I thanked her for how much she had invested in me and contributed to my success. She said, "When you can do for someone else what I've done for you, that is the highest thanks you can give me." It has taken me most of my career, but I have finally been able to thank her properly.

RESILIENCE INSIGHTS

- Mentorship is a symbiotic relationship that fosters resilience in both mentors and mentees. Mentors offer guidance, support, and wisdom based on their experiences, nurturing the growth of mentees. Simultaneously, mentors experience personal and professional growth through their role as guides and facilitators of learning.
- A key mentorship component is creating a safe space where mentees can openly discuss challenges, aspirations, and vulnerabilities. This environment of trust and confidentiality contributes to building

resilience by allowing mentees to seek guidance without fear of judgment, enabling them to confront difficulties more effectively.

- ·Transformational leaders who embrace mentorship empower their teams to become more resilient. By providing guidance, support, and opportunities for growth, these leaders help team members develop skills, gain confidence, and overcome challenges. This process contributes to building a team of leaders who can support each other and drive continuous improvement.

11

PASSING THE BATON

"A leader is like a shepherd. He stays behind the flock, letting the most nimble go out ahead, whereupon the others follow, not realizing that all along they are being directed from behind."

— *NELSON MANDELA*

L et me tell you a story:

Once, there was a wealthy man who was about to embark on a journey. Before leaving, he summoned his servants and entrusted them with his wealth. To one servant, he gave five talents; to another servant, he gave two talents; and to the third servant, he gave one talent. Each servant received according to their abilities. Afterward, the man went on his journey.

The servant who received five talents immediately went to work, investing the money and doubling its value, gaining five more talents. The servant who received two talents did the same, investing and gaining two more bags. However, the servant who received one talent became fearful. He dug a hole in the ground and buried his master's money, taking no action to grow it.

After a long time, the master returned and settled accounts with his servants. The servant who had received five talents presented the additional five bags he had gained. The master commended him, recognizing his faithfulness and diligence, and rewarded him with greater responsibility and joy.

Likewise, the servant who had received two talents came forward and showed his master the two additional bags he had gained. Once again, the master praised his faithfulness and rewarded him with increased authority and happiness.

However, the servant who had received one talent approached his master and returned the exact amount he had been given, explaining that he had hidden it out of fear. The master was disappointed with this servant's lack of initiative and laziness. He rebuked him for not at least depositing the money with the bankers to earn interest.

The master then took the one talent from the unproductive servant and gave it to the servant with ten bags. He explained that those who had demonstrated faithfulness and productivity would continue to receive more, while those who lacked initiative would lose even what they had.

This retells the parable of the talents found in the Gospel of Matthew in the Christian Bible (Matthew 25:14-30). Though it has religious origins, its underlying messages can be applied to many facets of life. I have shared it with you because I have always found it to be an excellent metaphor for transformational leadership, emphasizing the importance of proactive leadership, pushing boundaries, nurturing talent for organizational growth, and leading with courage and resilience.

I like to think of the servants as leaders entrusted with organizations. In this context, the talents represent an organization's leadership potential, talent, and resources. Transformational leaders, like the servants who received multiple talents, recognize the potential for growth and development. They actively invest their leadership abilities, empowering and inspiring their teams to reach new heights. These leaders push boundaries, encourage innovation, and create an environment where talent flourishes.

On the other hand, the servant who buried the talent can be seen as a representation of a leader who is hesitant to take risks and lacks the faith to drive change and growth. They may prefer to maintain the status quo, fearing the unknown and the potential challenges that come with pushing for more. As a result, the organization stagnates, lacking resilience and the ability to adapt to changing circumstances.

To me, this story highlights the importance of transformational leadership in driving organizational success. Effective leaders embrace their role as stewards of the organization, specifically of the team members they are charged with serving. Doing so creates a ripple effect, empowering individuals to become leaders themselves and propelling the organization forward in a cycle of continuous improvement. Last, the parable encourages individuals to make the most of the individual opportunities presented to them, whether large or small. The goal is to grow the team's talents and contribute to making the world a better place. Applying this parable, the servant leader focuses on the student and staff talents, and growing everyone's greatness is the most important mission.

I've titled this chapter "Passing the Baton" for several reasons. First, this book is about building resilience within yourself and within an organization or learning community. As we've discussed, that resilience comes from working with others and developing the leaders around you—like a relay captain training your teammates so that you can each run a strong leg. Here is one more analogy for you to think about. The world record for the men's 400-meter dash is 43.03 seconds, and the world record for the 4 x 100-meter relay is 36.84 seconds. What do you think has created such a huge difference?

In the 400-meter dash, each team has one runner, one

competitor running for the total 400 meters. This runner has to manage his speed and conserve his energy for the duration of the race. In the relay, each team has four runners sharing the burden of the race. Each one is allowed to run at their absolute best, knowing they will hand off the baton to their teammate, who will also run at their best. When that relay team has the most synergy, they go further faster because of the performance each runner can bring. This book is about helping you build your best relay team, developing runners who can propel the whole system forward and reach outcomes no one could reach alone.

The second reason is that this book is my way of passing the baton to you. I have worked in education for forty-two years. I've held various leadership positions and have had to work through all of the challenges each one entails. I have had to redefine leadership and resilience repeatedly to improve student outcomes and build teams that can keep moving forward without me.

Now I have reached a phase where the way I can best contribute to this cycle is to double down on my investment in you as a mentor and a guide. Each of you reading this book is set to face challenges I have not yet encountered as the world evolves. It is my hope that this book provides a framework for you to be successful through it all. The principles I have given you are not tactics to employ religiously but more of a strategy or mindset for guiding your approach to comprehensive problem-solving. To that end, let's take a look back at the concepts we have covered so you can solidify your understanding (or identify chapters you may want to go back to).

RETRACING OUR STEPS

In Chapter 2, we began exploring servant leadership as Robert Greenleaf explained. Servant leadership is a philosophy that prioritizes serving others over personal gain or organizational success.

It is especially crucial in education, as demonstrated during the COVID-19 pandemic. Servant leaders exhibit active listening, empathy, and healing, creating an environment for growth and development. They decenter themselves, empower the community, and bridge divides by listening to diverse perspectives and working collaboratively. By putting the needs of others first and focusing on the common good, servant leaders guide their organizations toward shared success and foster a positive impact on individuals and communities. This lays the foundation for understanding the role of servant leadership in school improvement and emphasizes the importance of turning the light from yourself to focus on the group's efforts.

In Chapter 3, we take that a step further to emphasize transformational leadership. Transformational leadership is a powerful style that goes beyond servant leadership by not only prioritizing the needs of others but also developing future leaders and fostering a culture of shared leadership. It involves second-order change, which requires a shift in values and beliefs beyond superficial adjustments. Transformational leaders lead by example, inspire others, and create a shared vision collaboratively pursuing solutions. It is about achieving results in a way that transforms the community, individuals, and the concept of leadership itself. This style emphasizes being less transactional or top-down in favor of empowering individuals to contribute their best skills and ideas, driving innovation and growth through continuous improvement.

Chapter 4 explains what continuous improvement is and how it works, drawing from and building on the work of Salina, Girtz, and Eppinga in *Powerless to Powerful*. The continuous improvement cycle involves three components: data, collaborative inquiry, and systems. Data serves as the foundation for informed decision-making and can be qualitative, quantitative, or triangulated. Collaborative inquiry is a process where teams of educators work together to investigate issues, analyze data, and develop action plans for improvement. Systems are established to monitor progress and sustain positive outcomes over time. The cycle is ongoing, with teams continuously collecting data, engaging in collaborative inquiry, implementing action plans, and monitoring progress. Resilience and shared ownership are key to the process, as teams need to work together effectively, overcome challenges, and maintain a focus on student learning. The continuous improvement process is illustrated through a real-life example of a school where technology was integrated to enhance literacy skills and inclusivity, resulting in positive outcomes. The chapter emphasizes the importance of resilience, finding positive outliers, and compounding momentum to drive continuous improvement.

Chapter 5 explores the concept of creative tension as a dynamic force that drives innovation. Creative tension is about closing the gap between the current reality and the desired outcome by creating a sense of urgency and motivation for individuals to take action, problem-solve, and continuously improve. The chapter emphasizes that creative tension is not about fixing problems but about identifying desired outcomes and using a timeline to generate faster innovation. Using collaborative inquiry to develop and test interventions and establishing feedback loops to monitor progress within a specific time window allows organizations to shorten the growth and improvement cycle through consistent monitoring and adjusting in a given timeframe. What is important to remember about continuous improvement and creative tensions is that you are *not* just looking at where students are struggling. You want to look for positive outliers and assess how you can get greater gains.

This leads us to Chapter 6's discussion of focus. Where we focus, we see growth. Chapter 6 emphasizes the importance of laser-focus in education and transformational leadership. By identifying subgroups of students, analyzing data, and designing targeted interventions, educators can close learning gaps in specific areas, maximize student potential and achieve equitable outcomes. Laser- involves being intentional, targeted, and precise, monitoring progress, and measuring success. Collaboration, data analysis, and resilience play key roles in developing and implementing targeted strategies. The risks of not being focused include wasted time and resources and learning gaps, but with laser-focus, you can raise the bar in your organization much more effectively and address the specific needs of students more thoroughly and quickly. The result is students are less likely to repeat the same errors and move forward with a stronger knowledge and foundation.

In Chapter 7, we delved into the significance of partnerships in education and how they can truly make a difference. Collaborating with schools, educators, students, families, community organizations, and businesses is vital for creating inclusive and supportive learning environments while embracing cultural diversity enriches children's growth and fosters an appreciation for different perspectives providing options to gather and value a broader community voice. We learned that raising and educating children is a collective responsibility that requires collaboration, cooperation, and active engagement from all stakeholders. Finally, we explored what is needed for partnerships to be successful for all parties involved.

Chapters 8 and 9 built on this with community voice and group goal-setting. Community voice and group goal-setting are fundamental aspects of effective collaboration in education. Community voice entails actively involving and meaningfully engaging all stakeholders, including parents, families, students, educators, and community members. It recognizes the value of diverse perspectives, experiences, and expertise in shaping educational practices and decisions. By embracing community voice, a more inclusive and empowering environment can be created where everyone's input is heard, respected, and taken into account. Group goal-setting involves collaboratively defining shared objectives and aligning efforts to achieve them. It enables stakeholders to collectively shape the direction and purpose of their collaborative endeavors, ensuring they address the specific needs and aspirations of the educational community.

Finally, Chapter 10 delved into the call to mentorship and the role of a leader in walking alongside others to reach their goals and purpose. It discussed the concept of readiness and the significance of establishing trust in relationships that respect and empower learners on their leadership journey.

REVEALING RESILIENCE

Throughout our journey together, we have touched upon the importance of resilience in leadership. I want to reiterate the importance of defining what resilience means for you in your new role:

Resilience Within

Resilience begins with a mindset that embraces change and uncertainty as opportunities for growth. It requires you to be open to new ideas, willing to step outside your comfort zone, and ready to learn from both successes and failures. By embracing a growth mindset, you can transform setbacks into valuable learning experiences and find the motivation to keep pushing forward.

An essential aspect of resilience is building solid relationships and networks of support. As a leader, surround yourself with individuals who inspire and uplift you, both within and outside your organization. Foster a culture of collaboration and mutual support among your team members, where they feel safe to share their challenges and seek guidance. By encouraging these connections, you create a support system that can help you navigate challenging times and find innovative solutions.

That leads us to another vital aspect of resilience: the ability to adapt and embrace change. The educational landscape is continuously evolving, and as a leader, you must be willing to embrace new approaches, technologies, and pedagogies. Emphasize a culture of continuous learning within your organization, encourage experimentation, and create opportunities for professional development to grow momentum and motivation for all stakeholders to find a place to use their talents and share their expertise. By embracing change and encouraging innovation, you can position your organization for success in the face of evolving educational needs.

To that end, you must maintain a sense of purpose and perspective as a resilient leader. Personally, remember the impact you are making on the lives of students and the educational community. Stay focused on your mission and core values, especially during challenging times. Recognize that setbacks and obstacles are temporary and view them as opportunities to learn, grow, and strengthen your leadership.

And last, keep in mind that resilience also involves self-care and self-awareness. Take time to recharge and nurture your physical, emotional, and mental well-being. Understand your strengths and limitations, and practice self-reflection to gain insights into your leadership style and decision-making. Never lose sight of what is truly important to you, and make important decisions based on your values and priorities.

By cultivating resilience, you enhance your ability to navigate challenges and serve as a role model for your team. Your resilience will inspire and empower others to persevere and find their own resilience. Together, you can weather any storm, overcome obstacles, and continue striving for excellence in education.

Resilience Without

Resilience in the system or organization provides opportunities for individuals within the organization to develop shared leadership and to go beyond the status quo, and extends to the preparation and empowerment of the entire team. As a transformational leader, one of your primary responsibilities is to build resilience by equipping the team to thrive in your absence. This begins by establishing a clear and compelling vision that guides the collective efforts and inspires a shared sense of purpose while building the skills sets to manage and monitor the organization in the team. By effectively communicating this vision and aligning it with the values and goals of the team, you create a solid foundation for resilience.

Furthermore, resilience is fostered through data-driven collaborative decision-making. As a leader, you involve the team in the process of analyzing data, identifying areas for improvement, and developing action plans. By actively seeking input, valuing diverse perspectives, and promoting shared ownership, you enable the team to make informed decisions and take collective responsibility for driving positive change. This collaborative approach strengthens the team's problem-solving abilities. It ensures a smooth transition of leadership, as individuals are already equipped with the skills and knowledge needed to carry the organization forward.

In addition to collaborative decision-making, building momentum with quick wins is essential for sustaining resilience. By focusing on achievable short-term goals and celebrating successes along the way, you create a positive and energized atmosphere within the team. Quick wins provide a sense of accomplishment and fuel motivation, building confidence in the team's ability to overcome challenges. This momentum serves as a catalyst for continuous improvement and empowers the team to adapt, innovate, and maintain resilience even in the face of adversity.

By nurturing a culture of collaboration, innovation, and continuous improvement, you lay the foundation for long-term resilience within the organization. As you pave the way for others, your role as a transformational leader is to ensure that the team is prepared, motivated, and inspired to carry on the mission and sustain success beyond your tenure. By investing in the growth and development of individuals, fostering a shared vision, and creating an environment of trust and empowerment, you enable the organization to thrive and adapt in an ever-changing landscape.

As you embark on your leadership journey, remember that building resilience is a continuous process. It requires ongoing self-reflection, learning, and adaptation. By developing resilience, you equip yourself with the tools and mindset to lead with confidence, compassion, and unwavering determination.

TO THE FUTURE

As we reach the conclusion of this book, I want to leave you with three important reminders that encapsulate the key principles we have explored together:

First, embrace your role as a servant leader. Make it a priority to serve others above personal gain or organizational success. Actively listen, show empathy, and foster an environment where growth and development can thrive. Strive to be a model of transformation and a transformer of the organization and those you lead. Go beyond meeting the needs of others and focus on developing future leaders. Lead by example, inspire those around you, and cultivate a culture of shared leadership that encourages innovation and continuous improvement.

Second, place a strong emphasis on continuous improvement.

Utilize data, engage in collaborative inquiry, and establish systems that inform decision-making and drive positive outcomes. Build resilience in the system by including everyone, and encourage growth by identifying positive outliers. Harness the momentum to propel your organization forward.

Third, remember that everyone is needed. The system is strengthened by diversity not uniformity. The test of a leader is to create union toward a shared purpose while respecting unique perspectives and individual dignity. Leadership is not about individual achievements; it is about serving the collective purpose of the group. The team rises as you strengthen its members, and you will rise as your team holds you and each other up.

As I pass the baton to you, I want to assure you that you are not alone on this journey. I have complete faith in your ability to face the challenges ahead and positively impact the lives of students and the educational community. I see your greatness and have given you this book to nurture it. *You* are a pearl, and today, I am polishing you to reflect light to others. May you find strength, balance, and fulfillment as you continue to grow and inspire greatness as you take this cloth (the tools and insight in my book) to polish others until they shine with their excellence and brilliance. The collective light shines on everyone; together, we can make a difference.

RESILIENCE INSIGHTS

- Resilience in leadership starts with cultivating a growth mindset that views challenges as opportunities for growth and learning. Embracing change and stepping out of comfort zones become pathways to acquiring new skills and perspectives. A resilient leader thrives on continuous self-improvement, turning setbacks into stepping stones toward success.

- Building resilience within an organization involves fostering a shared vision that unites team members and empowers them to weather uncertainties together. Collaborative decision-making enhances problem-solving capabilities and creates a sense of collective ownership. Celebrating small wins along the way boosts morale and sustains momentum for overcoming challenges.

- Embracing a servant leadership approach, leaders prioritize the growth and well-being of their team members. They create an environment of mutual support by actively listening, empathizing, and encouraging open communication. Incorporating continuous improvement practices driven by data and collaborative inquiry ensures adaptive and forward-looking strategies that reinforce both individual and team resilience.

ACKNOWLEDGMENTS

In crafting this message to my dedicated colleagues, many of whom have been instrumental in finding solutions and fostering learning in diverse international places, certain key leaders, teachers, and mentors have stood out in my career path. First, I want to express my gratitude to Margo Long, who ignited my passion for differentiated instruction early in my educational journey and supported me through my doctoral studies in critical thinking assessment. Second, I am deeply grateful for the leadership, mentorship, and friendship of Dr. Shirley Holloway over the past 35 years. Her diverse leadership, commitment to equity, and partnership development have been a guiding force in my experiences in Washington, Alaska, and Arizona.

Third, I must extend my thanks to Father Ford, Dr. Richard Wolfe, and my Gonzaga Doctoral Committee for believing in my capabilities and supporting me in achieving my goals. The Gonzaga University program's servant leadership and transformational organization approach have been foundational in my leadership preparation, enabling me to respond to opportunities and challenges on an international scale. My successful international experiences were made possible by the invaluable contributions of George Dymond, ISS at Princeton, Dr. Suzan Gerber, Susan Foglia, and numerous dedicated teachers and administrators representing diverse backgrounds, all of whom have significantly impacted my career and life path.

Fourth, I am grateful for my many colleagues and graduate

students, particularly Ted Howard and Dr. Chuck Salina, whose coaching experiences have been profoundly impactful. Their encouragement led to the publication of this book and the development and implementation of technology-supported instruction and leadership tools. Throughout my 42-year career, various professional leaders, including Aleene Quall, Dr. Melodee Loshbaugh, Michael Kirby, Dr. Larry Nyland, Dr. Debra Nieding, Dr. Sandi Wilson, Dr. Nancy Isaacson, Ambassador Delano Lewis, Geoff Lewis, Dr. Richard McBride, Dr. Gary Livingston, and Dr. Brian Talbott, have been instrumental in guiding and supporting my work.

On a personal level, my focus on faith and resilience has been shaped by my mother, whose belief in my adventurous spirit and ability to overcome challenges has been a driving force in my life. My sister Connie has been a role model, exemplifying the value of doing the right things. My daughter, Katrina Clauson, has profoundly influenced me with her fortitude and creativity, reminding me to continuously reinvent and embrace learning options to live life to the fullest.

I must also take a moment to extend my heartfelt gratitude to my exceptional editor and writing coach. Your guidance, support, shared learning, and unwavering perseverance have been instrumental in shaping this transformative process. Having you alongside me throughout this journey has been an incredible gift, and I deeply appreciate your commitment to bringing out the best in my work. Your keen insights and thoughtful feedback have enriched this book and elevated it to new heights. Thank you for being a valued partner in this endeavor and helping me share my message with the world in the most impactful way possible.

Last, I want to recognize all those who have engaged in conversations and collaborative efforts to transform schools and work environments for the betterment of future generations. From classmates who have been with me since childhood, keeping the focus on bringing out the gifts of others to colleagues who have fearlessly tried new strategies in their workplaces, I have been inspired by your commitment to making the world a better place through learning and growth.

—Cynthia L. Clauson

APPENDIX
ADDITIONAL READING

Below are additional resources you may find valuable as you continue your professional development.

Edgley, Ross. *The Art of Resilience: Strategies for an Unbreakable Mind and Body*. Harper Collins. 2020.

Greenleaf, Robert K. *The Servant as Leader*. Newton Center, Mass. Robert K. Greenleaf Center, 1970.

Greitens, Eric. *Resilience: Hard Won Wisdom for Living a Better Life*. Macmillan. 2015.

Hesse, Hermann. *The Journey to the East*. The Noonday Press, New York, NY, 1956.

Sendjaya, Sen; Sarros, James C. (September 2002). "Servant Leadership: Its Origin, Development, and Application in Organizations". *Journal of Leadership & Organizational Studies*.

REFERENCES

Clauson, C. & Myhre, O. "H.E.A.R.T. II." Curriculum in Context, 27 (1), 18-20, 2000.

Clauson, C. "In Search of Solutions: The H.E.A.R.T Diversity Technology Project." *Curriculum in Context*, 25 (1), 18-20, 1999.

Clauson, C. & Myhre, O. "H.E.A.R.T." Research project testing effectiveness of Light span - Achieve Now software with ESL students, 2000.

Etzioni, Amitai. "Moral Leadership: Getting to the Heart of School Improvement: An Executive Book Summary by Alex Bergerman." Web log. *EDUBLOG FOR LEARNERS* (blog), 2015. https://vuthedudotorg.files.wordpress.com/2015/06/moral-leadership-sergiovanni-ebs.pdf.

Fritz, Robert. *The Path of Least Resistance: Principles for Creating What You Want to Create*. New York City: Stillpoint Publishing, 1989.

Greenleaf, Robert K. *Servant leadership: A Journey into the Nature of Legitimate Power and Greatness*. 25th Anniversary ed. New York: Paulist Press, 2002.

Lewis, Delano. *It All Begins with Self: How to Discover Your Passion, Connect with People, and Succeed in Life*. Pasadena, CA: Best Seller Publishing, 2015.

Lewis, John, and Brenda D. Jones. *Across that Bridge: A vision for change and the Future of America*. New York: Legacy Lit, 2017.

Loshbaugh, Melodee, and Cindy Clauson. "Turning Straw into Gold." *WA ASCD Curriculum in Context* , no. Fall/Winter (1988): 22–24.

Sagor, Richard. *Guiding School Improvement With Action Research*. Alexandria, VA: Association for Supervision and Curriculum Development, 2000.

Salina, C., Girtz, S., & Eppinga, J. (2016). *Powerless to Powerful: Leadership for School Change*. Lanham, MD: Rowman & Littlefield.

Salina, C., Girtz, S., & Eppinga, J. (2016). *Transforming Schools Through Systems Change*. Lanham, MD: Rowman & Littlefield.

Salina, C. and Suzann Girtz. *Powerless to Powerful: Coaches' Handbook - K–12*. Washington Office of Superintendent of Public Intruction, 2019. https://www.k12.wa.us/sites/default/files/public/ossi/k12supports/pubdocs/Coaches%20Handbook%206-2019.pdf.

Sendjaya, Sen; Sarros, James C. (September 2002). "Servant Leadership: Its Origin, Development, and Application in Organizations". Journal of Leadership & Organizational Studies. 9 (2): 57–64.

Senge, Peter M. *The fifth discipline Fieldbook. The Art & Practice of Learning Organization*. 1st ed. New York: Currency & Doubleday, 1990.

Sergiovanni, Thomas J. *Moral Leadership: Getting to the Heart of School Improvement.* San Francisco: Jossey-Bass-Pfeiffer, 1996.

ABOUT THE AUTHOR

Dr. Cynthia Clauson is an educational leader, coach, instructor, speaker, mentor, and trainer. Her passion lies in helping readers develop leadership skills and streamline learning through holistic and individualized perspectives. Working with multiple teams, she has created critical thinking, solution-finding, and technology tools to support innovative learning methods. Cynthia's entrepreneurial focus centers on making learning accessible to children, parents, teachers, and leaders across various government, business, and university roles. This book encourages transparency, vulnerability, and confidence in discovering "Ah-ha" moments and achieving better results.

As a child, Cynthia was intrigued by teaching and unconventional thinking. While at Whitworth University, she explored ways to ignite passion and purposeful learning among her students. Initially, she discovered the link between critical thinking and the arts in music performance, leading her to develop tools for all learners. Her leadership studies at WSU and Gonzaga University refined her goal of implementing critical and creative thinking across diverse communities as a teacher and leader. Through hands-on coaching and technology-supported tools, Cynthia's leadership extended to various locations, including Washington, Alaska, Arizona, Washington DC, Qatar, and Bahrain. She tested her technology tools in leadership, training, and coaching roles, eventually becoming a research director for an online high school serving 33 States.

Driven to develop all learners' gifts, Cynthia served on the Arts Commission in Alexandria, VA, and collaborated with the Duke Ellington Performing Arts High School team in Washington, DC. These experiences connected her coaching journey with arts and global critical thinking. Cynthia's approach unites learning, leadership, and listening to transform individuals and communities, achieving shared greatness and tangible results.

Outside of work, Cynthia cherishes time with her pugs and daughter in Washington and Wyoming. She can be found in nature, walking her dogs, working out at the gym, and conversing with lifelong learners at beaches, coffee shops, or art experiences. Additionally, as a certified yoga instructor with Breathe for Change, she volunteers to develop community options for children across diverse backgrounds, embracing the value of engaging in different places and communities.

To connect with Cynthia, reach her at drclauson@gmail.com. As CEO of Educational Coaching Plus, PLLC, she offers consultation, coaching, speaking, and training engagements in education, government, business, civic, and university communities.